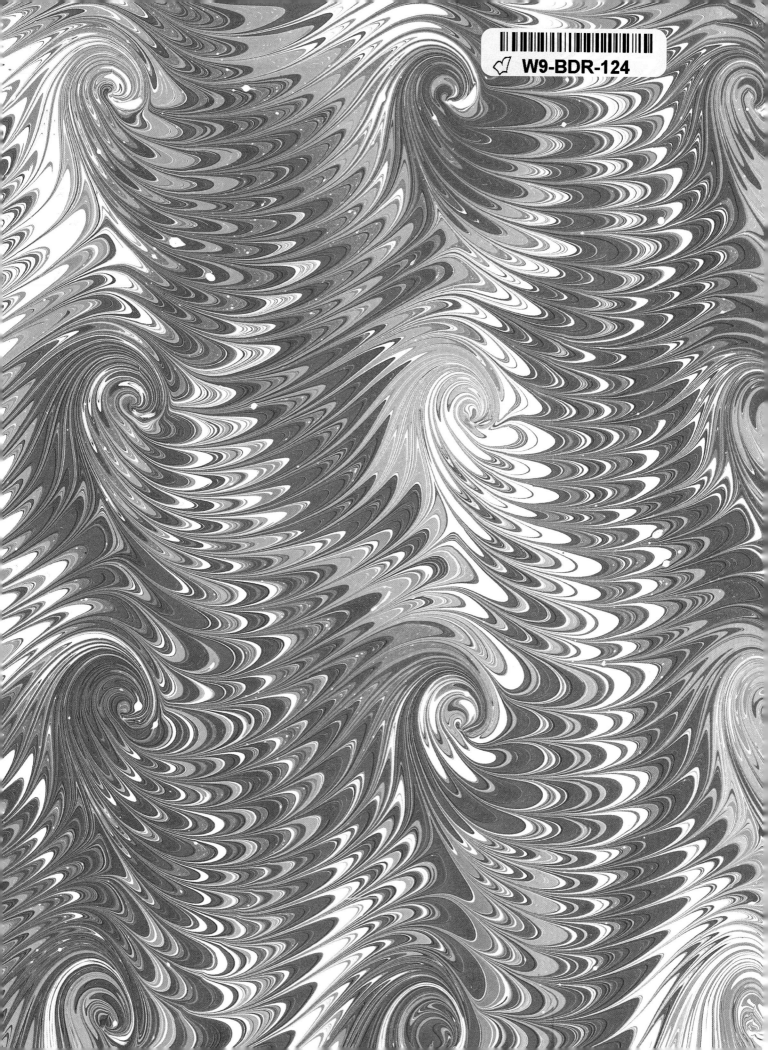

American PT Boats
In World War II
A Pictorial History

Victor Chun

American PT Boats

In World War II

A Pictorial History

Victor Chun

Schiffer Military/Aviation History
Atglen, PA

ACKNOWLEDGMENTS

With the fire at Elco's New Jersey plant several years ago and the dissolution of Higgins Industries in 1965, records and photographs concerning PT boats were either destroyed or disposed of. Therefore, all materials in this book had to be gathered painstakingly from private sources, museums and various departments of the government. To those individuals, who generously supplied me with unique stories and unusual photographs, I am most grateful.

I gratefully acknowledge my indebtedness to the following people for their courtesy and cooperation:

Admiral William C. Specht (retired), who was in charge of the MTB Training Center at Melville, Rhode Island, during the war, was most helpful with his technical knowledge.

The late "Boats" Newberry, his kindness during my visit to his PT Boat Museum in Memphis, Tennessee, enabled me to copy a large number of rare photographs.

Douglas Fairbanks, Jr., the famous actor, who in spite of his busy world wide activities, took the time to write me several long letters about his experience with PT boats in the Mediterranean.

George Sprugel, Jr., who sent me his enlightening story on the development of the torpedo rack.

James B. Stewart, an expert on post war PT boats having served aboard one during that period, furnished almost all the materials on that subject.

Joe Lavastida and the late Josh Sherman, who carefully read over the manuscript, and helped with editing the first edition.

Kathy Brawn for her help with editing the second edition.

Victoria Mary Chun, my young daughter, who accompanied and helped me on my many research trips, thus making my traveling less of a chore. She also single handedly transferred the manuscript and captions of the second edition to computer disk.

Susan Chun, my wife who helped in so many ways too numerous to name here.

To all others who had assisted me and not mentioned here, please accept my sincere thanks.

Cover artwork by Steve Ferguson, Colorado Springs, CO

PT 191 BAMBI AND BLOOM: By late 1943, the U.S. Navy had established a lethal force of PT boats in the Southwest Pacific theater, particularly at the forward base of Dreder Harbor on the Huon Peninsula of New Guinea. The PT squadrons assumed the grim task of interdicting enemy troop barges throughout the Solomon Sea area, resulting in an appalling execution of seaborne Imperial infantry.

Exemplary of the combat was the voyage of PT 191 BAMBI commanded by Ensign Ramsey Ewing (USNR, of Squadron 12 in support of the Cape Glouster, New Britain invasion. In the company of PT 190 JACK O'DIAMONDS commanded by Lt. Ed Farley, USNR). They were returning from their patrol area in the Vitiae Strait when Japanese dive bombers intervened. In a day long running battle, Farley's 190 was able to avoid damage within the safety of a low cloud bank, while the less fortunate BAMBI was destined to bear the worst.

The crew of PT 191 excelled. When Ewing was wounded, second officer Ensign Fred Calhoun (USNR) relieved him at the controls, and despite several near misses, he steered BAMBI safely through the falling bombs while the gunners shot down four of the attackers. Below decks, Motor Machinist Mate Victor Bloom secured the shrapnel damage to the engine room, doused fires and tended to the wounded, all the while maintaining BAMBI's engines at flank speed.

Bloom's resolute demeanor in the grave event resulted in his citation for bravery with the Navy Cross. Eventually, the crews of Squadron 12 and their campaign cohorts of Squadron 21 would be cited in a Presidential Dinstinguished Unit Citation, the only PT squadrons to be so honored in their theater. The cover depicts BAMBI during her epic fight.

DEDICATION

To Mother and Dad for the usual things and much more, much much more. Also to J.M. "Boats" Newberry, my mentor.

Book Design by Ian Robertson.

Copyright © 1997 by Victor Chun.
Library of Congress Catalog Number: 96-72151

Printed in the United States of America.
ISBN: 0-7643-0256-6

We are interested in hearing from authors with book ideas on related topics.

Published by Schiffer Publishing Ltd.
77 Lower Valley Road
Atglen, PA 19310
Phone: (610) 593-1777
FAX: (610) 593-2002
E-mail: schifferbk@aol.com
Please write for a free catalog.
This book may be purchased from the publisher.
Please include $2.95 postage.
Try your bookstore first.

CONTENTS

FOREWORD

Five decades after World War II, the heroic saga of the Patrol Torpedo Boat (PT Boat) begins to fade from our memories, even though their effectiveness and versatility were among the sensational in the annals of the United States Navy. The toll of enemy vessels taken by these speedy and reckless crafts is out of all proportion to their small size and relatively low cost. Although more than 800 PT boats were built in the United States during the war, only a few have survived the attrition of time.

To PT boat veterans, I hope this book will rekindle their nostalgic memories of those valiant years. To others, I hope it brings them a better understanding of these magnificent boats used by these intrepid crews throughout the war. Perhaps for a brief moment, we can return to those thrilling days of yesteryear and recall a fleeting wisp of glory. For one brief shining moment, we too can feel the salt spray on our faces and hear the deep-throated roar of the powerful Packard engines as the PT boats move out to make their rendezvous with destiny.

Victor Chun
2584 Wellesley Ave.
Los Angeles, CA 90064

INTRODUCTION

Twenty years have elapsed since the first printing of this book. In 1976, my book was the first nongovernment publication on the subject of PT boats. Only 1200 copies were printed. Most of the pictures in this book were used many times in later books by others. As more pictures and drawings were discovered, more materials were added to this second and enlarged edition. For example, the original profiles and deck plans of PT 810, 811 and 812 are the only ones in existence. The previously published diagrams of tactics and formations were specifically declassified for me in order to be included in the first edition.

It was my intention to keep the text in this book to a minimum for it is primarily a visual presentation of the subject. The praise and accolade, so deserving of the PT crew, were also omitted. This was done not to minimize their importance, but because they were

covered adequately in other books and magazines. I recommend *At Close Quarters* by Robert J. Bulkley, Jr. (U.S. Government Printing Office, 1962) for further reading. It covers the development and combat history of the PT boats admirably.

The effectiveness and versatility of the PT boats were among the sensations in the annals of the United States Navy. They had more hours of actual combat with the enemy than any other type of ship.

The types of PT boats used in the Navy during World War II were the Elco 77 and 80 footers and Higgins 78 footers. Their hulls were constructed of laminated mahogany with over 400,000 screws and glue to hold them together. Three Packard marine engines of 1500 hp. each powered the boats which had three screws and three rudders. Total fuel tank capacity was 3000 gallons of 100 octane

Ink drawing of Lt. Ken Sharpe's PT 327, which took part in the Battle of Surigao Strait. Courtesy of Ken Sharpe.

War time painting of a PT boat created by the Elco art department to promote the Elco boats. Courtesy of Elco.

aviation gasoline. The total weight of the boat was approximately 55 tons.

PT boats operated from either a Tender or an island base. Both had experts to service the boats with engine overhaul, hull repairs, and replenishment of torpedoes and ammunition. The crew usually consisted of two officers and 12 enlisted men. Later, as more and heavier armament was added, the crew was increased to as many as 18.

Usually 12 boats made up a squadron. There were 43 commissioned squadrons in World War II operating in all theaters of operation: South Pacific, Aleutians, Philippines Islands, Panama, English Channel and Mediterranean.

The armament of PT boats consisted of a 40 mm Bofors cannon aft, twin .50 cal. machine guns in the port and starboard gun turrets, a 20 mm Oerlikon and a 37 mm automatic gun forward, depth charges, four torpedoes, small arms and hand grenades. Mortars and rockets were added later.

PT boats were used as ambush vessels, hunters, marauders, spy transports, rescue boats, escort, ferrying, barge sinking, beach head invasions and seeking out and destroying enemy ships.

During the writing of the first edition, I corresponded with Admiral William C. Specht, who was in command of the PT Boat Training Center, as well as other PT boat officers and men to insure the accuracy of my writing. Still, mistakes were discovered after publication. The worst of which were the picture of the Packard engine printed upside down and the "doctored" picture of PT 103 captioned as PT 109.

In spite of my diligence, mistakes will be made in the second edition. I will accept full responsibility and welcome any new information you care to send me. Only then, the ultimate truth can finally be attained.

Proudly she waved, the PT boats carried her from the South Pacific to the English Channel.
"May the God we trust as a nation
Throw the light of His peace and grace
On a flag with its stripes untarnished,
And with every star in place. (John Clair Minot). *Courtesy of Michael Kalausky.*

1

PEARL HARBOR
(Squadron 1 and 17)

The PT boats of Squadron 1 under way next to the USS Hornet, off Pearl Harbor. Courtesy of the National Archives.

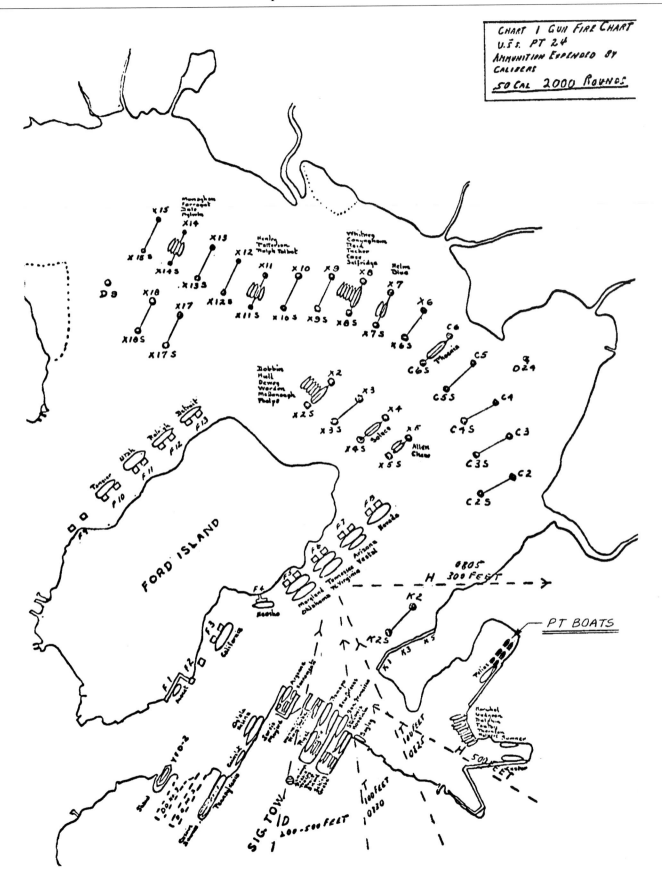

Diagram included in the combat report to the Commander-in-Chief of the U.S. Pacific showing the disposition of the fleet and PT boats on December 7, 1941. Courtesy of C.W. Faulkner.

Elco 77 foot PT boat cruising off Pearl Harbor. Note the covered Lewis machine gun on the forward deck. Courtesy of the National Archives.

PT 20 of Squadron 1, with pre-war markings, making a test run before shipping to Pearl Harbor. This boat saw action on December 7, 1941. Courtesy of the National Archives.

Refueling at Pearl Harbor prior to the long trip to Midway, PT 28, together with the other boats of Squadron 1, ran from Pearl Harbor to Midway, a distance of almost 1400 miles, under their own power. They were refueled by a seaplane tender enroute. This was the longest run that PT's had ever made. Courtesy of the National Archives.

2

THE PHILIPPINES
(Squadron 3)

During those hectic early days of the war, no combat photographers were on hand to record the daring exploits of the PT boats in the Philippines. Later, drawings were made based on the experiences of the PT boaters. This is one of the few paintings done at that time. Courtesy of Packard.

OPPOSITE: On April 8, 1942, Lt. Robert B. Kelly, the squadron executive officer on board PT 34, at the eastern side of Cebu, encountered a Japanese light cruiser. Under heavy fire, two torpedoes were fired. Seen through binoculars by Kelly, two spouts of water appeared amidships. Courtesy of the Warner Research Center.

PT 41, Squadron 3, skippered by Squadron Commander Lt. John D. Bulkekey, played a major role in the Philippines campaign. General MacArthur and his family were "taken out of the jaws of death" on board this boat. Later, Manuel Quezon, President of the Philippines Commonwealth, was also "rescued" on board PT 41. The end of PT 41 came on a steep mountain road to Lake Lanao. It was hauled there to prevent Japanese float planes from landing. As a Japanese force was closing in, PT 41 had to be destroyed. Courtesy United States Navy.

During the sea action at Subic Bay, PT 32, one of the six PT boats at the Philippines, appeared to damage a Japanese minelayer. It finally became unseaworthy and was abandoned and destroyed by gunfire from the United States submarine PERMIT to avoid capture. Courtesy of the United States Navy.

3

MIDWAY

PT 42 of Squadron 1 on patrol off the coast of Midway. On June 4, 1942, the brief encounter between PT boats and Japanese fighters resulted in the destruction of one low flying Zero. Courtesy of the National Archives.

The new Elco 77 foot PT boats, arriving too late for the Battle of Midway, patrol the coast. Courtesy of the National Archives.

Oil storage tanks and hanger burning after the Battle of Midway, June 4-7. PT 22 of Squadron 1 is in the foreground. Courtesy of the Bonte via PT Boat Museum.

Just before sunset on June 10, 1942, after the conclusion of the Battle of Midway, two PT boats left the coast to embark on a unique burying mission. Each boat bore two wooden coffins adorned with the insignia of the rising sun. To be buried were four Japanese naval aviators who had crashed on Midway. As the sun settled gradually down the vast expanse of the ocean, dispersing its majestic rays across the Pacific sky, the PT boats moved slowly out to deep water with their flags at half mast. After the services were read by a chaplain, three volleys were fired by the Marines. The coffins were then lowered gently overboard. When men die bravely for their country, even though their cause may be wrong, they sometimes are buried with full military honors when the conditions of war permit. Painting by Lt. Commander Griffith B. Coale. Courtesy of Esquire, Incorporated.

4

THE SOLOMONS

(Squadron 2,3(2),5,6,9,10,11,13,19,20,23,27,28,31,32 and 37)

A PT boat cruising in Tulagi Harbor. Right after the successful landing of the United States Marines on Guadalcanal and Tulagi on August 7, 1942, the PT boats set up their first base at Tulagi. They engaged in nightly battles with the Japanese cruisers and destroyers, known as the Tokyo Express, coming down the "Slot." Courtesy of the National Archives.

On the morning of July 20, 1943, three zebra striped PT boats of Squadron 10 were strafed by four B 25 medium bombers. The PT boats fired at the planes thinking they were Japanese. One B 25 was hit and crashed. All three boats were hit and PT 166 caught fire and burned. Courtesy of the PT Boat Museum.

The aftermath of the encounter between PT boats and B 25's. Courtesy of the PT Boat Museum.

The Elco 77 footer (left) and the 80 footer (right) on board the S.S. Stanvoc Capetown sailed from New York to Brisbane, Australia at the end of 1942. Courtesy of William C. Quinby.

PT 107 of Squadron 5 saw action at the Solomons. She was destroyed by fire at the dock when the exhaust blast lighted the gasoline on the water due to a defective valve in the fuel line. Courtesy of the United States Navy.

PT 121 of Squadron 6 arrived in the South Pacific in time for the last actions with the Tokyo Express at Guadalcanal. Courtesy of William C. Quinby.

The only known picture of PT 109 with numbers showing. It was being transhipped on board the S.S. Joseph Stanton to the South Pacific. Courtesy of Warner Research Center.

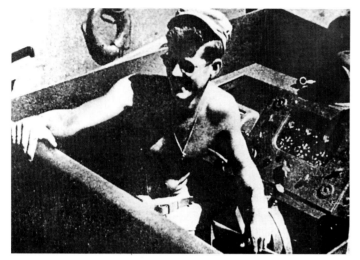

PT 109 on a mission off Guadalcanal. Courtesy of the Warner Research Center.

Lieutenant John F. Kennedy relaxed at the cockpit of his PT 109 of Squadron 2 based at Rendova. Courtesy of the Warner Research Center.

Three different views of the early Elco PT boats underway somewhere in the Pacific. Note the lack of radar dome on top of the flage mast.

PT 59, September 1943, at Tulagi just after it was put in commission. Lt. Kennedy sits in the cockpit. Courtesy of the Warner Research Center.

PT 103 getting a refueling line from the USS Pocomoke (AV-9). PT 103 was south of LT. John F. Kennedy's PT 109 in Blackett Strait on the night the PT 109 was rammed by the Japanese destroyer AMAGIRI. Courtesy of the National Archives.

Lt. Liebenow's PT 157, the boat that picked up Lt. Kennedy from a native canoe near Patparan and later picked up his crew on Olasana. Courtesy of the PT Boat Museum.

A Higgins boat, first used by Squadron 13. Courtesy of the National Archives.

PT 174, Lt. Russel W. Rome, fired four torpedoes at the Japanese destroyer and observed two explosions near the Kolombangara shore. Note the extra 40 mm gun at the bow. Courtesy of the Warner Research Collection.

Lt. Charles Tilden (PT 43), a typical young skipper of a PT boat in the South Pacific. He saw plenty of action at Iron Bottom Bay, attacking the Tokyo Express at night. On the night of January 2, 1943, his boat was hit by a Japanese destroyer, forcing the crew to abandon ship. One enlisted man was killed and 2 were missing. Tilden became squadron commander on March 1, 1944 and was awarded the Commendation Ribbon. Courtesy of the United States Navy.

5

THE ALEUTIANS
(Squadron 1,13 and 16)

PT boats based at Adak, in the middle of the Aleutian chain. The Aleutian weather is known to be the worst in the world. Courtesy of the United States Navy.

PT boats patrolling the sea to keep the enemy from sending reinforcements. Courtesy of the National Archives.

PT boats in the Aleutians, sharing the sea with a PBY Catalina. Courtesy of the United States Navy.

Stationed at Attu, the PT boats were shepherded by a seaplane tender which supplied them with ammunition, fuel and repair service. They maintained a vigilant patrol in the cold waters of our northern outposts. Courtesy of the National Archives.

Close-up view showing the intricate mechanism of the 40 mm gun usually mounted at the stern of the PT boat by strengthening the after deck. It was most effective in blowing up enemy barges.

6

NEW GUINEA

(Squadron 2,7,8,9,10,11,12,13,16,17,18,20,21,23,24,25,28,33 and 36)

PT Boat with native scouts on board at base in Morobe. Courtesy of the National Archives.

PT 196, "Green Dragon," of Squadron 12 was operating from Kiriwina, on the south coast of New Britain. On March 12th and 13th, 1944, Lt. Alfred G. Vanderbilt in PT 196 and LT. Cyrus R. Taylor in PT 193 shot down a Japanese floatplane. Courtesy of Buscher.

OPPOSITE: Screened by the overhanging trees and the camouflage they have added, the crew lived in bases they had hewed out of the jungle with the aid of natives of New Guinea. Courtesy of the National Archives.

PT 337 of Squadron 24 was destroyed by enemy shore batteries at New Guinea. One Shell hit the tank compartment and went through the engine room. The boat burst into flames and exploded after the crew got into the life raft. Courtesy of the National Archives.

TOP: PT 337 (Ens. Henry W. Cutter) of Squadron 24 was heading into Hansa Bay, New Guinea on March 7, 1944. An enemy shell hit the fuel tank compartment and went through the engineroom. All three engines were knocked out and the tank burst into flames. The crew abandoned ship and got into the small raft. After three days of agony from exposure, the five survivors, including Ens. Cutter, were picked up by a Catalina flying boat on the morning of the 11th. BELOW: A HIGGINS 78' PT boat underway somewhere in the Pacific. Courtesy of the National Archives.

Late in the afternoon of June 26, 1944, PT 130 (New Guinea Krud), covered by Australian Beaufighters, made four daytime firing runs on 15 Japanese supply barges at the coast of Muschu Island. Six were ablaze and four explosions followed. PT 130 returned to the tender, took on fresh supplies and came back after dark. The PT boat made four more runs, completing the destruction of all 15 barges. Courtesy of the United States Navy.

PT 144 of Squadron 8 returning from a long night mission after sinking several enemy barges and pulling free another boat that went aground on a reef. Note the white stripes around the bottom of the radar dome which all Squadron 8 boats carried. Courtesy of Earle P. Brown.

PT 328 of Squadron 21, which was awarded the Presidential Unit Citation for action in the New Guinea area. Courtesy of M. Kalausky.

PT 149 patrols off the coast of New Guinea to catch any enemy barges. On the night of July 28th and 29th, 1943, PT 149 with PT 142, ran into a flotilla of thirty or more barges. One tried to ram PT 149, but the PT sank it when it was only ten feet away. PT 149 was hit by a 20mm shell in the engine room. After quick repair, it was able to return to Morobe. Courtesy of the United States Navy.

40 mm gun crew on PT 331 ready to open fire to cover the landing of troops by LCVs and LCMs at Tong Islands. Courtesy of the National Archives.

7

THE MEDITERRANEAN

(Squadron 15,22,34 and 35)

PT boat on board oiler ENOREE arrived and unloaded at Gibraltar on April 13, 1943. Courtesy of E. DuBose.

PT 208 off loading U.S. tanker ENOREE at Gibraltar, April 23, 1943. Courtesy of E. DuBose.

PT boats on oilers arrived and unloaded at Gibraltar in April, 1943. Courtesy of E. DuBose.

A PT boat with striped camouflage at Salerno Bay. Courtesy of the National Archives.

Two PT boats near an LST during operations at Salerno, Italy. Note the PT boat in the foreground camouflaged with stripes. Courtesy of the United States Navy.

A PT boat lays a smoke screen around the invasion force at Salerno, Italy. Courtesy of the United States Navy.

Prior to the invasion of Sicily, Squadron 15 staged in Lake Bizerte, outside of Karouba Air Base. Courtesy of E. DuBose.

Lt. Douglas Fairbanks, Jr. aboard PT 303, en route to base at the island of Vis on the Dalmatian coast. He was returning from a mission to set off rockets and smoke pots at different beachheads to confuse the enemy as to the actual landing spot. Courtesy of the PT Boat Museum.

PT 557, one of the four boats equipped with Thunderbolt gun mount. During night patrol, the continuous tracers streaming from the Thunderbolt gun, like the beam of a searchlight, can hurl destructive projectiles (20 mm) at 1800 rounds per minute at the enemy. Courtesy of M. Kalausky.

PT boat base at Bastia, Corsica, just inside the seawall. From here the entire Gulf of Genoa was within easy patrolling distance. Courtesy of M. Kalausky.

Squadron 15 boats in Bastia Harbor. The shark teeth belonged to PT 203. Lt. Robert Reade was the boat captain. Courtesy of E. DuBose.

Squadron 15 boats in Bastia Harbor. New Mk 13 torpedo on launching rack in left foreground. Courtesy of E. DuBose.

During the invasion of Southern France, one fully loaded glider, accidentally released from the towing plane, hit the water with a splash and floated with the wing above water. On board PT 562, which was standing by during the rescue operation, Seaman 1st Class Michael Kalausky took this picture. Courtesy of M. Kalausky.

PT boat base at Bastia just inside the seawall. Courtesy of M. Kalausky.

PT 215 headed for patrol out of Bastia. Notice new MK 13 torpedoes on stern using the open launching rack. The forward torpedoes are the old style MK 8 torpedoes with the very heavy compressed air launcher. The cannon on the stern pad is an army 40 mm. There is a single 20 mm pointing up. Two twin 50 caliber machine guns are in the bridge turrets and a 37 mm British anti-tank gun is on the bow. Smoke generators are the cylinders on both sides of the stern. There is a single barrel .30 caliber machine gun mounted on the port torpedo tube. Courtesy of E. DuBose.

Squadron (Ron) 15 Higgins Boat departing on patrol against German supply lines along the Italian Coast. The Germans were using "F" Lighters and Italian ships to supply the German army along the Southern front of Italy. Convoys originated from Savona, Genoa and La Spezia. Courtesy of E. DuBose.

PT 558, which took part in the invasion of Elba, is armed with an Elco Thunderbolt gun. Courtesy of the United States Navy via Charles Minton.

PT 559, equipped with the Elco Thunderbolt, a power driven mount holding four 20 mm cannons, was commanded by Lt. Robert E. Nagle. It sank a German corvette with one torpedo at a 400 yard range on the night of September 13th and 14th, 1944, near Genoa Harbor. Courtesy of E. DuBose.

Lt. Eugene S. A. Clifford's PT 204 was damaged after ramming a German minesweeper during a patrol near Genoa. Courtesy of E. DuBose.

PT 212 at floating drydock at La Maddalena, off the North Coast of Sardinia. Courtesy of the United States Navy.

Higgins PT 211, with rocket launchers, in Bastia Harbor, Corsica, Italy. Courtesy of the United States Navy.

Manufactured by the Higgins Boat Company in New Orleans, this Higgins Boat was probably on an acceptance run in Lake Ponchartrain. There are no torpedoes, guns or depth charges. In fact, there is no U.S. Navy furnished ordinance on the boat. Courtesy of E. DuBose.

This is USN Chief Motor Mechanic Frenchie Dusett directing the installation of a rebuilt engine package in a Squadron (Ron) 15 Boat at the Karouba Base in Bizerte, North Africa, Tunisia. This was an air base for French seaplanes. After Rommell surrendered, Ron 15 established a major overhaul base, Repair Base 12, using the abandoned aircraft hangers and quarters. This was also the staging base for the invasion of Pantelleria and later Sicily. Courtesy of E. DuBose.

Left, Lt. Norman Hickman. Courtesy of E. DuBose.

This is the advanced operating base for Ron 15-22-29 at Bastia, Corsica. This photo is of Ron 15 taken during the Fall of 1943. Courtesy of E. DuBose.

Left, Lt. John Mutty, Center, Lt. (JG) Dick O'Brien, Right, Lt. Cdr. Stanley Barnes. Stanley Barnes, Squadron Commander of Ron 15 and finally Commander of Ron 15-22-29 which were named as a task unit. John Mutty was Exec. Off. of Ron 15. Dick O'Brien was Boat Captain of PT 205 and then Division Commander. The picture was taken outside of the Squadron Office at Madellena Island Base. All three officers were graduates of the Naval Academy. Courtesy of E. Dubose.

Ron 15 Boats nested in Bastia Harbor. The paint on the bow was part of identification for friendly aircraft. The bow had a 4 foot wide yellow stripe and the stern a 4 foot wide red stripe. Courtesy of E. DuBose.

Squadron 15 Higgins boat tied up to the Blue Grotto on Capri during the battle for Naples in September, 1943. Courtesy of E. DuBose.

Lt. Edwin A. DuBose of Squadron 15 at the Mediterranean was awarded the Navy Cross, Silver Star and Distinguished Service Cross (British) "For extraordinary heroism in action as a commander of a Division of Motor Torpedo Boats engaged in operations against enemy coastal traffic off the west coast of Italy in March and April 1944. The exceptional heroism, intrepidity and outstanding devotion to duty displayed by Lieutenant DuBose were in keeping with the highest traditions of the Naval Service." Courtesy of E. DuBose.

8

THE ENGLISH CHANNEL

(Squadron 2 (2) and 30)

PT 199 carrying Admiral Harold R. Stark to invasion beachhead in France. On D Day, PT boats took part as screen forces in the invasion of Normandy and escorted minesweepers to clear a sea lane to the beaches. Courtesy of the National Archives.

A PT boat escorts ships transporting salvage units to Cherbourg. Courtesy of James A. Nicholson via PT Boat Museum.

PT 509 assisted in the rescue after USS TIDE, a mine sweeper, was hit by a magnetic mine planted by German E boats near St. Marcouf. The PT boats, with their wooden hulls and shallow draft, were the only vessels that could move safely through magnetic minefields. However, four United States PT boats were destroyed by acoustic and pressure mines. Courtesy of the National Archives.

PT boats of Squadron 34 at the wharf at Portland Bill, England, the Royal Navy's torpedoes base. There they got their "fish." Courtesy of Squire.

British motor gun boats and American PT boats at the wharf at Portland Bill after D Day. Courtesy of Squire.

PT 313 Squadron 22 taken off from the coast of France, 1944. Courtesy of Bill Hindle.

PT 504, Squadron 34, placed in service January 11, 1944 took part in picking up survivors of destroyer escort RICH two days after D Day. Courtesy of the United States Navy.

9

THE PHILIPPINES (return)

(Squadron 8,9,10,12,16,17,18,20,21,23,24,25,27,28,31,33,36,38,39 and 40)

PT 191 refueling while underway between Palau and the Leyte Gulf. Courtesy of the National Archives.

Ensign Peter R. Gadd's PT 131 preparing for the upcoming battle of Surigo Strait. During the battle, PT 131's radar picked up the advancing Vice Admiral Shoji Nishimura's task force. Courtesy of the National Archives.

During the start of the Battle of Surigao Strait, a 4.7 inch shell knocked the 37 mm gun completely off its mount on the bow of Lt. (jg.) Joseph A. Eddins' PT 152, fatally wounded the gunner, stunned the loader and set fire to the boat. After the fire was put out, the boat still made 24 knots back to base. Courtesy of the United States Navy.

Lt. (jg.) Donald Maley's PT 106 leaving base at Mindoro for patrol duty. On May 15, 1945, it shelled three Japanese PT's hidden in the cove at Northern Davao Gulf and set them on fire. Courtesy of Earle P. Brown.

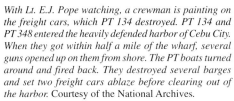

With Lt. E.J. Pope watching, a crewman is painting on the freight cars, which PT 134 destroyed. PT 134 and PT 348 entered the heavily defended harbor of Cebu City. When they got within half a mile of the wharf, several guns opened up on them from shore. The PT boats turned around and fired back. They destroyed several barges and set two freight cars ablaze before clearing out of the harbor. Courtesy of the National Archives.

During amphibious operations on Mindoro, PT boats were also used in the rescue operation after a LST was hit by a Japanese suicide plane. Courtesy of the United States Navy.

PT boat base at Mindoro, Philippines. Courtesy of the PT Boat Museum.

PT 523 rescued Ens. Crandell at Leyte. On the evening of October 27, 1944, PT 523 was on patrol north of Leyte in a heavy rain. Four Japanese planes bombed and strafed the boat. Eight men aboard were killed, three officers, six men and a war correspondent were wounded. Courtesy of the United States Navy.

Crew of PT 330 at Subic Bay, March, 1945. Courtesy of Reeks.

"February, 1945, we had been on patrol in Manila Bay the night before, and we stayed until daylight. Coming out of Manila Bay between Corregidor and Bataan Peninsula we saw two people in the water. The Japanese on the left was one of them.

They kept their backs turned to us as we approached and drifted up to them. When we were close, we called to them. At that time they turned to face each other, each held the head of the other under water, trying to drown each other.

When this did not work, the other man took a knife out of his waistband, plunged it into the left side of his abdomen and pulled it across to the right side. He then tried to hand the knife to the man on the left in the picture, but the knife slipped from his hand and sunk as he tried to pass it. We took aboard the survivor.

A few miles further, still heading west, we picked up the Japanese on the right. He was a nice, little, inoffensive fellow.

On the way back to Subic Bay they were held, hands bound, on the foredeck. The one on the left crawled across the deck and put his temple up against the carbine being held on them by one of the crew sitting on the 20 mm ready box on the starboard side forward of the chart house. He was asking to be killed.

As I said, the one on the right was a gentler man. Just after this picture was taken, he pulled out of his pocket a straight razor, barber scissors, and comb, and offered to stay with us as our barber.

I guess we did not search him very well.

Lt. Newcomb is indicating to the prisoners they should smile for the camera." *Photo and story courtesy of E.H. Duke Reeks.*

Cluster of PT boats lashed together near their tender for refueling and repair at Leyte, Philippines. Courtesy of the National Archives.

On the afternoon of December 10, 1944, PTs 323 and 327 were underway at Leyte Gulf for patrol station when four Japanese planes attacked them. As PT 327 turned one way, PT 323 turned the other way. One plane crashed into PT 323 admidship, damaging the boat beyond repair. Lt. (jg.) Herbert Stadler, the boat captain, was killed; Ens. William I. Adelman, the second officer, was missing; 11 men were wounded. PT 327, under the command of Lt. Ken Sharpe, picked up the survivors. Courtesy of E.H. Reeks.

PT 234 off the Coast off Mindoro, Philippine Islands. Courtesy of Charles H. Lake, Executive Officer of PT 234.

PT boat service insignia outside the operation hut of Squadron 3, the first to reach the Solomons. PT Boat Museum.

PT boats and paratroopers at Corregidor. Painting by Dwight C. Shepler. Courtesy of the United States Navy.

General MacArthur is shown arriving at Corrigidor aboard PT 373 on March 2, 1945. On the right is General Carlos P. Romulo, commanding General of the Philippines' forces. Courtesy of the United States Air Force.

*PT 525, with General Douglas MacArthur on board, ready to head for Tacloban, Leyte, on October 24, 1944. The boat captain of PT 525 was Lt. Alexander W. Wells,
USNR.* Courtesy of the PT Boat Museum.

General Douglas MacArthur aboard PT 525 which took him ashore at Tacloban, Leyte. Lt. General Walter Krueger, Commanding General Sixth Army, is shown beside him. Courtesy of the United States Navy.

Japanese prisoners picked up by a PT boat near Tarakan Island. Courtesy of the National Archives.

Burning of PT boats at Samar Island after World War II. Courtesy of K.L. Simmons.

PT 620 made a trial high speed run out of Sasebo Harbor, Japan, just before she was turned over to the South Korean Navy. Courtesy of the National Archives.

South Korean PT boats at Chinhae. Courtesy of R.F. Murray.

10

EARLY DEVELOPMENT

Fogal Boat Yard, Inc. built the 58 foot PT 1 and PT 2 based on Professor George Crouch's design for Henry B. Nevins, Inc. Courtesy of the PT Boat Museum.

Fisher Boat Works built the 58 foot PT 3 and PT 4 based on the same design as PT1 and PT2. Courtesy of the PT Boat Museum.

In 1939, Higgins Industries, Inc. received a contract to build the 81 foot PT 5 and PT 6 of the Sparkman and Stephens design. Courtesy of the National Archives.

The aluminum hull 81 foot PT 7 and PT 8 were built by the Philadelphia Navy Yard based on the Bureau of Ships' design. Courtesy of the Bureau of Ships.

The Scott-Paine 70 foot boat was purchased from England by Elco and subsequently designated PT 9. Courtesy of the PT Boat Museum.

PT 9 was modified to United States Navy configuration. It was placed in service with PT 3, on July 24, 1940, in Squadron 1. Courtesy of the PT Boat Museum.

PT 10 to PT 19 were built by Elco based on the Scott-Paine design at $220,000 each, using three Packard 1200 HP, V 12 marine engines. Courtesy of the PT Boat Museum.

PT 20 was the first larger 77 foot boat to carry the four standard 21" diameter torpedo tubes. During a comparative service test known as the Plywood Derby, PT 20 came in first with an average speed of 39.72 knots for the 190 mile course. Courtesy of the PT Boat Museum.

The Huckings PT 95 of Squadron 4, which was the training squadron at Melville, Rhode Island. None of the Huckins boats were used in combat. Courtesy of the Bureau of Ships.

The different hull design of the Higgins boat, as compared to the Elco, enabled it to run in heavier sea. it could also turn tighter making it more maneuverable. However, the Higgins could not match the speed of an Elco boat. Courtesy of the National Archives.

After the two sea trails, known as the "Plywood Derbies," the Navy wanted a heavier and longer boat. Elco built the 80 foot type, a different design from the 77 foot type, as the standard boat from this point on. Courtesy of the PT Boat Museum.

11

CONSTRUCTION

After getting the go ahead signal from the Navy, the assembly and production schedule of the Elco PT boats worked so smoothly that almost every boat was not only delivered ahead of contract time, but also exceeded all performance requirements. A rather unique method of hull construction saved many hours in assembly.

Hulls were built bottom up, then turned over and the engines were installed. The cabin, deck, superstructure and equipment were then added. Like airplanes, the PT boats were assembled on production lines from prefabricated components. The pictures following illustrate the construction of PT boats.

Modern wartime
production line

L. MACINTYRE

Courtesy of Elco

HULL CONSTRUCTION SEQUENCE

Courtesy of the United States Navy.

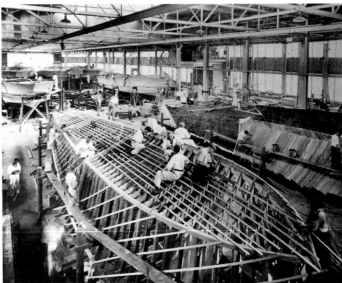

70 foot PT boat's main shop - looking north. Courtesy of Elco.

First stage - hull construction. Courtesy of Elco.

Courtesy of Elco.

Courtesy of Elco.

Courtesy of Elco.

Courtesy of Elco.

Section of main shop - looking north. Courtesy of Elco.

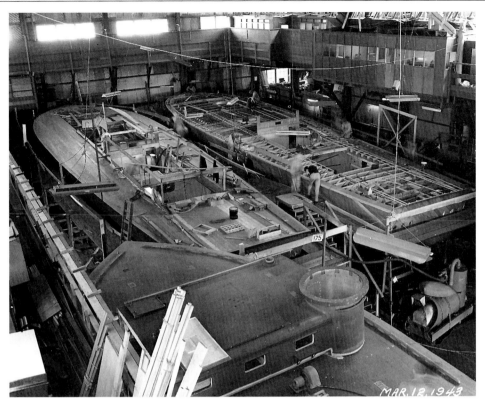

After the hull of the boat was completed, the decking was installed. In the foreground, the almost completed day room canopy with attached gun turret rested temporarily on the bow of another boat. Note the beautiful workmanship on these boats. Courtesy of the Bureau of Ships.

77 foot PT boats under construction. Main shop - looking east. Courtesy of Elco.

PT-103
ELCO BOAT WORKS
- First of 80 foot type -
4-21 in. Bow LAUNCHING
Tubes. Depth CHARGES
Alternate.

The PT 103, by Elco Boat Works, making a trial run. The testing of each boat after production was meticulous. Literally thousands of trials were run on hundreds of boats. For each run over the measured course, over 40 different readings, such as manifold pressures, change of trim, position of the bow wave, helm angle, accelerations and relative air speed, were recorded. Also, there were many special trials to test every possible improvement. Courtesy of the PT Boat Museum.

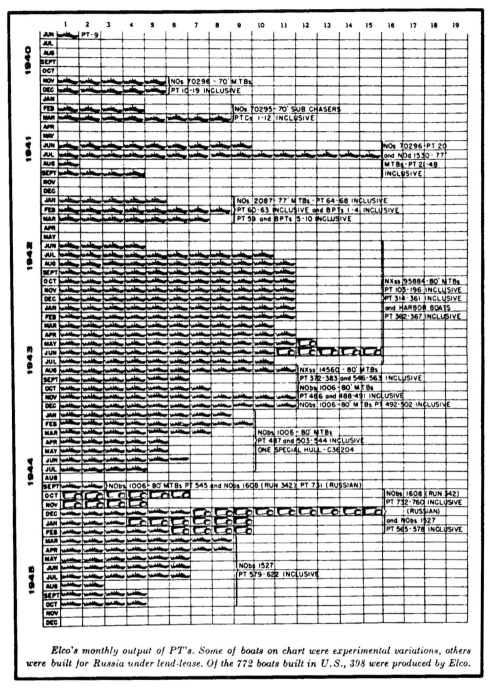

Elco's monthly output of PT's. Some of boats on chart were experimental variations, others were built for Russia under lend-lease. Of the 772 boats built in U.S., 398 were produced by Elco.

This chart displays the total output of Elco PT boats during World War II. Courtesy of Elco.

The Elco "slipper" was installed at the stern of this boat in 1945 for trial. Note the three mounting struts which hold it in place. It was designed to improve the boat performance by helping it plane more easily. It was not adopted as standard installation. Courtesy of the Warner Research Center.

A rare photograph of Mr. Henry R. Sutphen, Executive Vice-President of Elco. He went to England in 1939 to purchase the Scott-Paine boat, which was later designated PT 9. Courtesy of Elco.

OPPOSITE:Throughout World War II, variations of three types of PT boats were used in combat. They were Elco 77 footers, Elco 80 footers and Higgins 78 footers. Different views of these boats are shown here. Courtesy of the United States Navy.

12

ANATOMY OF PT BOAT

ELCO 80'

Courtesy of Robert Ferrell.

Courtesy of Robert Ferrell.

Courtesy of Robert Ferrell.

Courtesy of Robert Ferrell.

HIGGINS 78'

Higgins Industries, Inc
New Orleans, La.

PT 625 Class
STERN VIEW FROM ABOVE
Contract NObs 1680
3/1/45

Both photos courtesy of the PT Boat Museum.

Higgins Industries, Inc
New Orleans, La.

PT 625 Class
BOW VIEW FROM ABOVE
Contract NObs 1680
3/1/45

PT 297 saw action at Mindoro, December 1944. Note the heavy compressed air launchers on top of the torpedo tubes. Courtesy of the PT Boat Museum.

HUCKINS

Huckins PT boat practices laying a smoke screen. Courtesy of the National Archives.

PT 95 at Jacksonville, Florida. Courtesy of the Bureau of Ships.

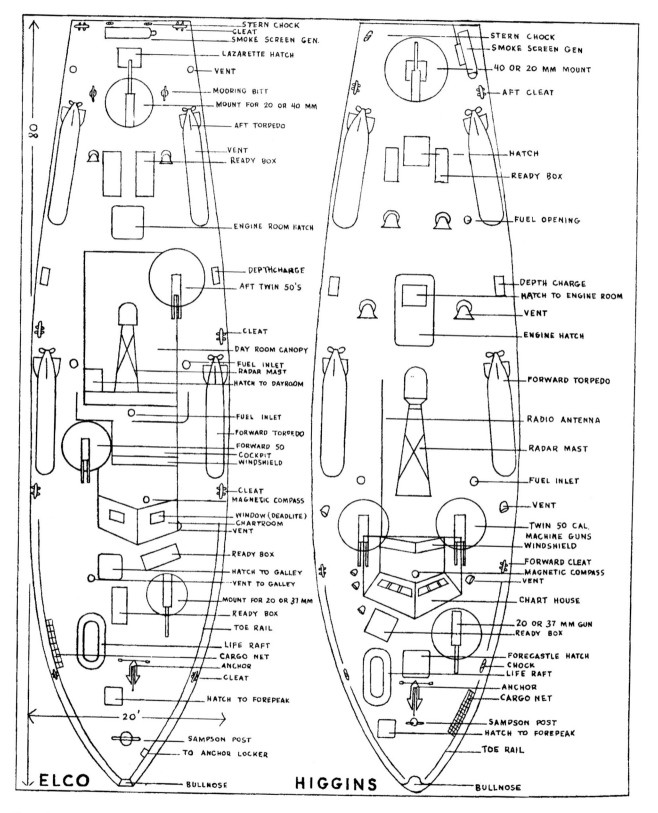

Elco and Higgins boats were the two main types used. This side by side drawing clearly shows the different deck arrangement of the two boats. Courtesy of the PT Boat Museum.

Mounted at the center of the bow is the 37 mm gun on a Mark 1 Mount with two boxes of ammunition behind it. Further back is the 20 mm gun with its drum magazines on top of their storage box. Both guns are especially effective in dealing with the enemy supply barges. The hatch to forepeak is located on the deck just in front of the 37 mm gun. At both sides of the chart-house are Mark 50 launchers, each with eight rocket launching tubes used mostly for shore bombardment. The life raft is stored on top of the chart-house. The PT boat number is painted on the front of the chart-house and the side of the .50 caliber machine gun turret. Courtesy of the Robert Ferrell.

The bridge, or cockpit, was the only area of the boat protected by steel armor plates. The officers, in fairness to the men stationed outside the bridge, had the armor plates removed to boost morale. Inside the cockpit is the instrument panel. The three gauges on top are tachometers that indicated the rpm of each engine. The gauges at the bottom indicate manifold pressure. The panel left of the gauges is the control for firing torpedoes. The electrical box just right of the steering wheel is the connection to the radio for sending and receiving on the bridge. The throttles for the engines are located just to the right of the gauges. Three compasses are mounted in the cockpit. They are not too dependable except in a calm sea. The door at the right leads to the chart house. To get the boat underway, the skipper should first make certain that the three throttles are in neutral. Then he signals the machinist's mates below in the engine room to start the engines and run them at idling speed. A seaman moves forward and aft to cast off the lines. The skipper then slowly advances the three throttle knobs with the heel of his palm. The engine-telegraph slot just ahead of each throttle changes from neutral to ahead which signals the engine room to shift gears. The needle on the RPM dial creeps higher as the PT boat swings out from the dock into the bay. The speed of the boat can now be adjusted by moving the throttle knobs. The seamanship of the skipper is determined by how he manipulates the throttle and the steering wheel.

The Interior of the bridge of a Higgins 78 footer. 1. Flux gate compass, 2. Pioneer compass, 3. Announciator and throttle, 4. Instrument panel, 5. Speaking tube to chart house, 6. Torpedo director stand, 7. Signaling searchlight, 8. Remote control. Courtesy of the PT Boat Museum.

Just to the right of the bridge is the forward twin .50 caliber machine gun turret. The tubular limit stop around the turret is to prevent the guns from shooting up the boat. Courtesy of Robert Ferrell.

At the extreme right side of the bridge is the bridge blinker key (with cover opened). It is used to send light signals. Courtesty Elco.

To increase fire power, a 40 mm gun is mounted at the stern to replace the 20 mm gun. Courtesy of Robert Ferrell.

The cylinder next to the 40 mm gun is a smoke generator. Courtesy of the Robert Ferrell.

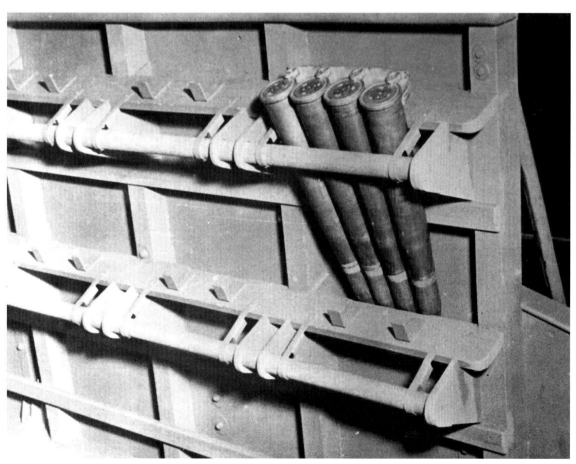

OPPOSITE: Close-up view showing detail of the twin .50 caliber machine guns turret. Note the steel rod frame the guns are mounted on. Courtesy of the National Archives.

ABOVE: 40 mm ammunition racks aboard PT 174. Courtesy of the Warner Research Center.

Higgins Industries, Inc.
New Orleans, La.

PT 625 Class
ROCKET LAUNCHER AND 37MM
Contract NObs 1680
3/1/45

5" Rocket launcher and 37mm gun are mounted at the bow of a Higgins boat. The latter were the same type of gun used in the Bell Airacobra (P-39) aircraft. Courtesy PT Boat Museum.

Close-up view of 37 mm shells used on board late model PT boats. The shell with black color projector denotes armor-piercing (A.P.) and the pointed projector denotes high explosive (H.E.). Both could be fitted with tracer for observation of fire. The 37 mm M4 cannon, built by American Armament Company (originally for P 39 aircraft), incorporated a 30 round magazine, and had a rate of fire of 150 rounds per minute. Courtesy of the PT Boat Museum.

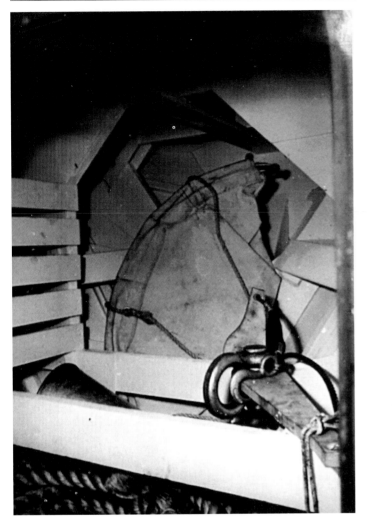

Forepeak showing sea anchor. Courtesy Robert Ferrell.

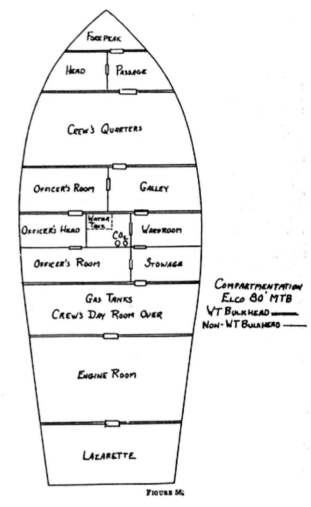

FORE PEAK

HEAD | PASSAGE

CREW'S QUARTERS

OFFICER'S ROOM | GALLEY

OFFICER'S HEAD | WATER TANKS CO_2 | WARDROOM

OFFICER'S ROOM | STOWAGE

GAS TANKS
CREW'S DAY ROOM OVER

ENGINE ROOM

LAZARETTE

COMPARTMENTATION
ELCO 80' MTB
WT BULKHEAD ———
NON-WT BULKHEAD ———

FIGURE 86;

Drawing of compartmentation of Elco 80 footer. Courtesy of the United States Navy.

Crew's quarters starboard aft showing lockers and berths. Courtesy of Robert Ferrell.

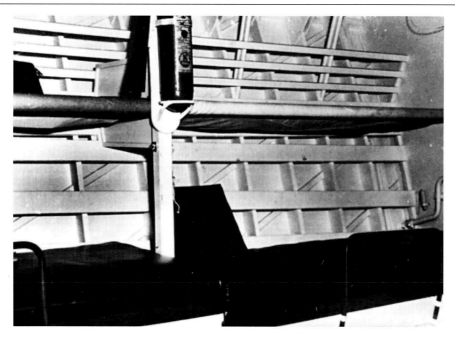

Crew's quarters berths close-up. Courtesy of Robert Ferrell.

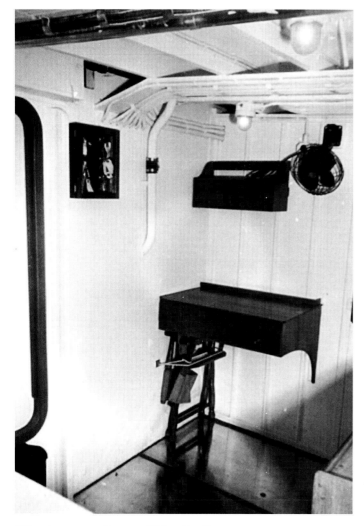

Officers' state room. Courtesy of Robert Ferrell.

Officers' head. Courtesy of Robert Ferrell.

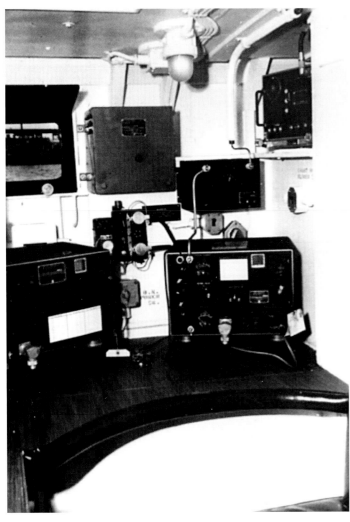

Radio installation in chart room. Courtesy of Robert Ferrell.

Close-up of radio receiver. Courtesy of Elco.

Radar equipment at forward starboard corner of chart room. Courtesy of Robert Ferrell.

Auxiliary compass in chart room. Courtesy of Robert Ferrell.

Engine room looking forward. Electrical panel at left of ladder. Courtesy of Robert Ferrell.

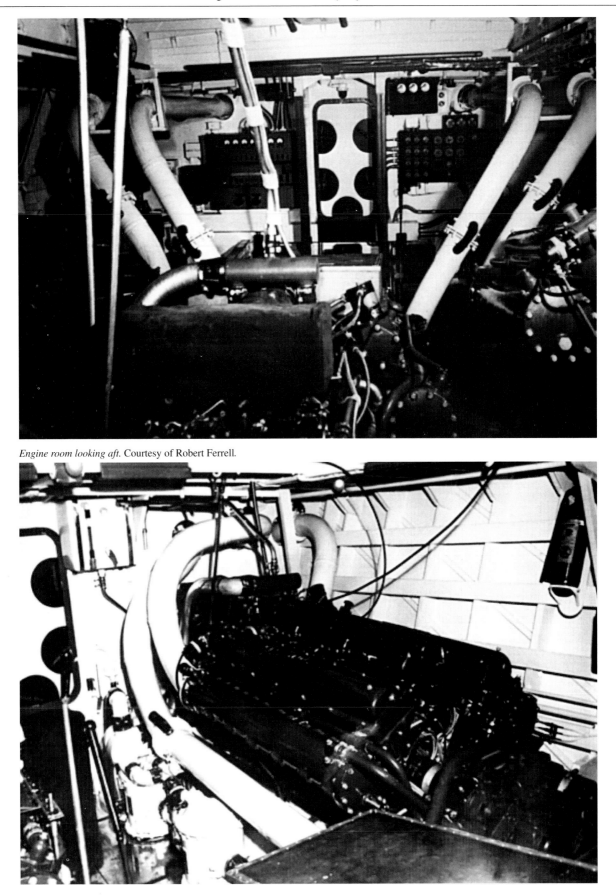

Engine room looking aft. Courtesy of Robert Ferrell.

Engine room port aft showing exhaust stacks. Courtesy of Robert Ferrell.

Starboard engine general view. Note seat for engineer at the top of engine and shifting levers. Courtesy of Robert Ferrell.

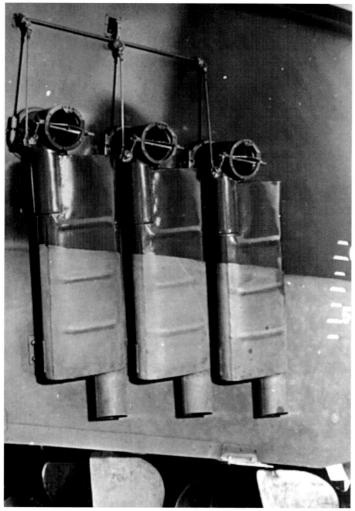

To decrease the noise of the three powerful Packard engines, six mufflers were installed at the stern of the boat. The linkages above the three mufflers could either direct the exhaust gas through the mufflers under water or straight out to increase power. Courtesy of Elco.

A close up view of the searchlight and the antenna mount. Courtesy Elco.

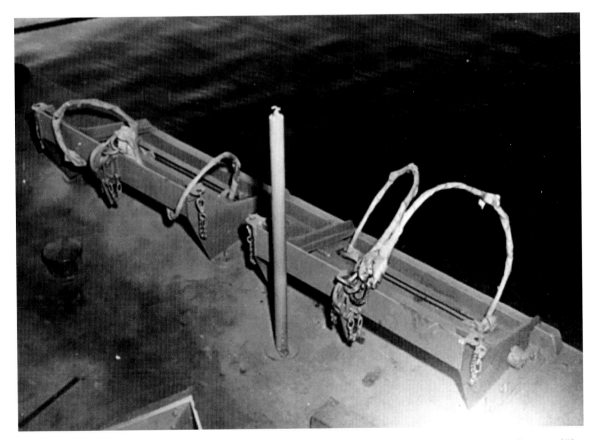

Sometimes the aft torpedo tubes were replaced with the depth charge racks. Depth charges are not shown in this picture. Courtesy of Elco.

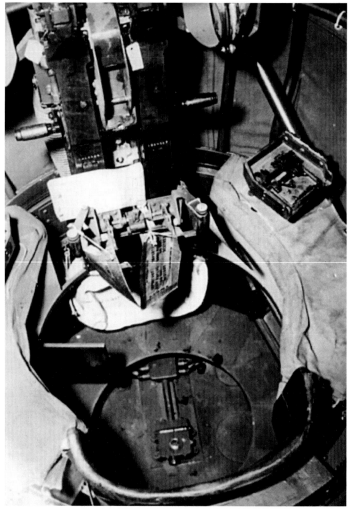

The PT boat usually operated at night. Therefore, radar was an extremely important piece of equipment in locating enemy ships. A close up view of the radar mast shows the detail of the radar reflector and rotating power unit. Courtesy of Robert Ferrell.

This is what the inside of the machine gun turret looks like. Courtesy of Robert Ferrell.

Cut-away profile view of Elco 80 footer. Courtesy of the PT Boat Museum.

<u>PT 20 type - PT's 20-68</u> (Elco Boatworks). Length 77 feet; beam 19'11"; draft 4'; displacement 35 tons.

(a)   Guns: Four .50 caliber air-cooled machine guns in two twin, hand operated scarf ring mounts. One .45 caliber Thompson submachine gun. One or two Lewis machine guns mounted forward. Two .30 caliber Springfield rifles. Thirteen .45 caliber Colt Automatics.

(b)   Ammunition: .50 caliber - 10,000 rounds per gun. .45 caliber - 4,000 rounds. .30 caliber - 1,200 rounds.

(c)   Torpedoes: Four 21 inch Mark 8-3C and D, speed 27 knots, range 13,500 yards.

(d)   Torpedo Tubes: Four 21 inch Mark 18-1 bow launching.

(e)   Depth Charges: Eight Mark 6 (300 pound charge).

(f)   Depth Charge Racks: Eight individual side launching type "C" or two (four charges each) stern launching.

(g)   Smoke screen Generator: Mark 3, capacity 32 gallon F.S. mixture.

(h)   Fresh Water: 180 gallons in two 90 gallon tanks.

(i)   Fuel: 3,000 gallons high octane gasoline.

(j)   Lubricating Oil: 30 Gallons.

(k)   Fresh Provisions: Four days' rations for nine men and two officers.

(l)   Communications: Blinker tube, semaphore, M.P. signal light, 8-inch searchlight, GF5, RU7 or TCS voice radio sets, range about 75 miles.

(m)   Radio Direction Finder: One R.D.F. per division.

(n)   Machinery: main engines - three 1,200 hp, Packard 4-M2500. Generator - 1 Lawrence 5-kw generator, air cooled. Power - four 6 volt storage batteries. Shaft - three shafts, three propellers (all right hand). Rudders - three rudders, mechanical steering.

(o)   Cruising Radius: Full load maximum speed, 41 knots, 259 miles. Full load maximum sustained speed, 35 knots, 358 miles. Full load one engine, 11 knots, 1050 miles.

After the PT boat reached the war zone, the additional equipment and armament installed were limited only by the ingenuity of the crew and what they could get their hands on. Some PT boats at the Solomons had all their torpedo tubes removed and installed two 40 mm guns fore and aft, along with four additional twin .50 caliber machine guns. Other boats had bazookas installed on board (see picture). The standard equipment furnished with each type of boat is listed on the following pages. Courtesy of the National Archives.

Elco lightweight 20 mm mount. Courtesy of the National Archives.

2. <u>PT type - PT's 71-94</u> (Higgins Industries). Length 78 feet; beam 20'8"; draft 5'3"; displacement 35 tons.

(a)   Guns: Four .50 caliber air cooled machine guns in two twin, hand operated scarf ring mounts. One 20 mm Oerlikon mount. One .45 caliber Thompson submachine gun. Two .30 caliber Springfield rifles. Thirteen .45 caliber Colt Automatics.

(b)   Ammunition: 20 mm - 1200 rounds. .50 caliber - 10,000 rounds per gun. .45 caliber - 4,000 rounds. .30 caliber - 1,200 rounds.

(c)   Torpedoes: Four 21 inch Mark-3C and D, speed 27 knots, range 13,500 yards.

(d)   Torpedo Tubes: Four 21 inch Mark 19 bow launching.

(e)   Depth Charges: Eight Mark 6 (300 pound charge).

(f)   Depth Charge Racks: Eight individual side launching type "C."

(g)   Smoke Screen Generator: Mark 3, capacity 32 gallon F.S. mixture.

(h)   Fresh Water: 200 gallons.

(i)   Fuel: 3,000 gallons high octane gasoline.

(j)   Lubricating Oil: 30 gallons.

(k)   Fresh Provisions: Four days rations for nine men and two officers.

(l)   Communications: Blinker tube, semaphore, M.P. signal light, 8 inch searchlight, TCS voice radio set, range about 75 miles.

(m)   Radio Direction Finder: One R. D. F. set per boat.

(n)   Machinery: Main engines - three 1,200 hp Packard 4-M2500. Later increased to 1,500 hp. Generator -two 1/2-kw water cooled generator. Power - four 6 volt storage batteries. Shafts - three shafts, three propellers (all right hand). Rudders - three rudders, mechanical steering.

(o)   Cruising Radius: Full load maximum speed, 41 knots, 259 miles. Full load maximum sustained speed, 35 knots, 358 miles. Full load one engine, 11 knots, 1050 miles.

20 mm Oerlikon gun mounted at the stern of the PT boat. It was replaced with a 40 mm gun on later boats. Courtesy of the National Archives.

PT 95 type - PT's 95-102 (Huckins Yacht Corporation). Length 78 feet; beam 19'5"; draft 5'; displacement 34 tons.

(a)   Guns: Four .50 caliber air cooled machine gun in two twin, hand operated scarf ring mounts. One 20 mm Oerlikon mount. One .45 caliber Thompson submachine gun. Two .30 caliber Springfield rifles. Thirteen .45 caliber Colt Automatics.

(b)   Ammunition: 20 mm - 1200 rounds. .50 caliber - 10,000 rounds per gun. .45 caliber - 4,000 rounds. .30 caliber - 1,200 rounds.

(c)   Torpedoes: Four 21 inch Mark-3C and D, speed 27 knots, range 13,500 yards.

(d)   Torpedo Tubes: Four 21 inch Mark 19 bow launching.

(e)   Depth Charges: Eight Mark 6 (300 pound charge).

(f)   Depth Charge Racks: Eight individual side launching type "C."

(g)   Smoke Screen Generator: Mark 3, capacity 32 gallon F.S. mixture.

(h)   Fresh Water: 200 gallons.

(i)   Fuel: 3,000 gallons high octane gasoline.

(j)   Lubricating Oil: 30 gallons.

(k)   Fresh Provisions: Four days rations for nine men and two officers.

(l)   Communications: Blinker tube, semaphore, M.P. signal light, 8 inch searchlight, TCS voice radio set, range about 75 miles.

(m)   Radio Direction Finder: One R. D. F. set per boat.

(n)   Machinery: Main engines - three 1,200 hp Packard 4-M2500. Generator - two 1/2-kw water cooled generator. Power - four 6 volt storage batteries. Shafts - three shafts, three propellers (all right hand). Rudders - three rudders, mechanical steering.

(o)   Cruising Radius: Full load maximum speed, 41 knots, 259 miles. Full load maximum sustained speed, 35 knots, 358 miles. Full load one engine, 11 knots, 1050 miles.

A single 40 mm cannon was installed at the stern of later PT boats. It was most effective to use against enemy barges. Courtesy of the National Archives.

PT 103 type - PT's 103-196 (Elco Boatworks). Length 80 feet; beam 20'8"; draft 5'; displacement 38 tons.

(a) Guns: Four .50 caliber air cooled machine guns in two twin, hand operated scarf ring mounts. One 20 mm Oerlikon mount. One .45 caliber Thompson submachine gun. Two .30 caliber Springfield rifles. Thirteen .45 caliber Colt Automatics.

(b) Ammunition: Same as PT 20 type.

(c) Torpedoes: Four 21 inch Mark-3 and D, speed 27 knots, range 13,500 yards.

(d) Torpedo Tubes: Four 21 inch Mark 18-1 bow launching.

(e) Depth Charges: Eight Mark 6 (300 pound charge).

(f) Depth Charge Racks: Eight individual side launching type "C."

(g) Smoke Screen Generator: Mark 3, capacity 32 gallon F.S. mixture.

(h) Fresh Water: 200 gallons.

(i) Fuel: 3,000 gallons high octane gasoline.

(j) Lubricating Oil: 30 gallons.

(k) Fresh Provisions: Four days rations for nine men and two officers.

(l) Communications: Blinker tube, semaphore, M.P. signal light, 8 inch searchlight, TCS voice radio set, range about 75 miles.

(m) Radio Direction Finder: One R. D. F. set per boat.

(n) Machinery: Main engines - three 1,200 hp Packard 4-M2500. Later increased to 1,500 Hp. Generator -two 1/2-kw water cooled generator. Power - four 6 volt storage batteries. Shafts - three shafts, three propellers (all right hand). Rudders - three rudders, mechanical steering.

DEVELOPMENT OF THE TORPEDO RACK

Experiments to develop new launching techniques were initiated at the Motor Torpedo Squadrons Training Center, Melville, Rhode Island, some time in 1942. One of the devices was based on the idea of hanging the torpedo in a life boat davit-like mechanism so that the torpedo could simply be dropped over the side of the PT boat. Because the PT Boat was not a very stable craft in rough seas, the device was not successful. Courtesy of the PT Boat Museum.

One night, in late February, 1943, Lt. George Springel, Jr. and Lt. (jg) James Costigan of PT 188 were in a Manhattan bar discussing a torpedo that a crew could slide and roll into the water. This was contrary to accepted doctrine which warned of the dangers of the gyro tumbling in the steering mechanism. Based on a few sketches made in a pocket notebook that evening, a prototype model of a torpedo rack was fabricated in the Scrap Metal Section of the New York Navy Yard. The design of the rack was simply that of an over-sized depth charge rack with greased skids. It was modified with a series of cables attached to a manually operated handle such that when the handle was pulled, it started both the gyro mechanism and the engine of the torpedo. After a brief delay to enable the gyro and engine to achieve full speed, the pins securing the torpedo in the rack were removed, and the torpedo simply slipped and rolled overboard. A few weeks following the construction of the prototype, it was installed aboard PT 188 when she was ordered to Newport on a weekend training exercise. With a borrowed Mark XIII torpedo with exercise head, testing was done at the Navy's torpedo firing range in Narragansett Bay. Over a period of several days, the torpedo was launched, recovered, serviced and launched again with complete success. A Navy Captain from the Bureau of Ordinance in Washington was just visiting the station and came along on several of the test firing runs. By the time PT 188 had returned to the New York Navy Yard, orders had been received from the Bureau to install this torpedo rack on all Squadron 12 boats. Courtesy of the National Archives.

HULL CONSTRUCTION

The construction of the 80 foot Elco PT boat starts with the assembly of the main frames, placed upside down, on a building jig. The frames are built of laminated spruce, white oak and mahogany. All the joints are secured with marine glue and screws. Both sides of the frames are covered with fir plywood to make it water tight. When finished, they are called bulkheads.

The keel, which is made of spruce, is then attached to the frames, spliced to the stem and secured with brass bolts. The chine, which is the hull member joining the bottom of the hull to the sides of the boat, is also bolted on. Longitudinal battens, running parallel to the chine, give further support to the planking.

The planking, which is the skin of the hull, is in two layers made of mahogany boards six inches wide laid diagonally opposite to each other, with sheets of airplane fabric and marine glue in between. The planks are fastened to the frames with screws and to battens with copper nails. When planking is completed, the hull is turned over and the inside work and decking begin.

The deck, like the planking, is also made of two layers of mahogany board with marine glue and airplane fabric in between. Both deck and planking are then bolted to a single continuous wooden member the entire length of the hull. The deck houses are built of spruce frames and covered on both sides with plywood. The space between the frames in the superstructure is insulated with cork.

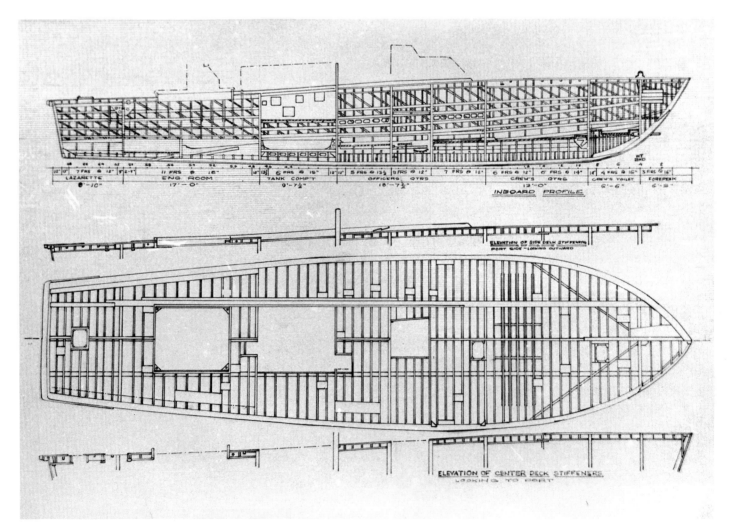

Hull framing of Elco 80 foot PT boat. Courtesy of the PT boat Museum.

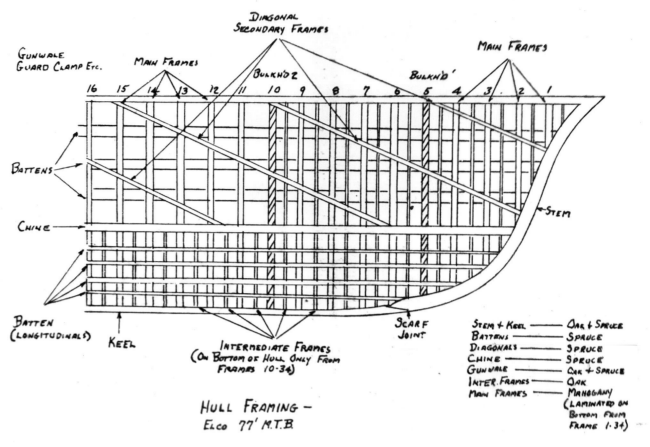

Forward hull framing of Elco 77 foot PT boat. Courtesy of the United States Navy.

ENGINE

The decision to use Packard engines in the PT boats began when Colonel J.G. Vincent, the designer of Packard's famous Library motor, became interested in PT boats. Elco specified the performance characteristics and left it to Packard to develop the marine engine. The result was a success in every respect, not only in performance but also in terms of manufacturing and production considerations as well. The development of this reliable power plant contributed much to the excellent overall performance of both the Elco and Higgins boats. The general specifications of the Packard engine are listed below:

Model -	4M-2,500
number of cylinders -	12
Fuel -	100 Octane gasoline
Cooling -	fresh water
Supercharger -	gear driven, centrifugal
Starter -	24 volt, electric
Generator -	28 volt, 40 amp
Bore and stroke -	6-3/8" x 6-1/2"
Rating -	1350 hp at 2400 rpm
Total piston displacement -	(2950)3 inches
compression ration -	6.4 to 1
Weight -	2950 lbs

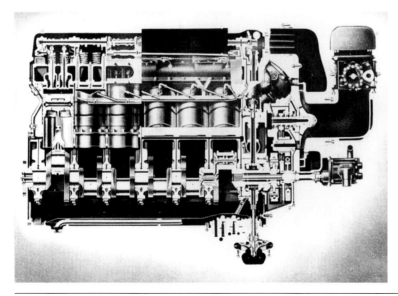

Cross section of Packard 4M-2500 type W-14 marine engine. Courtesy of PT Boat museum.

ONE-ENGINE OPERATION

R. p. m.	Knots	Gallons per hour	Cruising radius
700	8. 3	17. 5	1, 420
800	9. 5	22. 5	1, 270
900	10. 3	28. 8	1, 070
¹ 1, 000	11. 1	31. 7	1, 050
1, 100	11. 8	30. 2	903

TWO-ENGINE OPERATION

800	11. 8	45. 8	772
900	13. 2	62. 5	633
1, 000	14. 7	70. 8	623
1, 100	17. 0	75. 8	672
¹ 1, 200	19. 3	80. 8	718
1, 300	21. 5	87. 5	740
1, 400	23. 5	100. 8	704
1, 500	25. 1	120. 8	625

THREE-ENGINE OPERATION

700	10. 4	46. 6	669
800	12. 8	72. 5	531
900	15. 2	81. 7	558
1, 000	17. 2	100. 0	516
1, 100	19. 4	107. 5	542
1, 200	21. 8	129. 2	505
1, 300	25. 0	140. 0	536
1, 400	27. 2	145. 8	560
1, 500	28. 4	162. 5	534
1, 600	29. 5	175. 0	506
1, 700	32. 4	183. 3	530
1, 800	33. 2	200. 0	498
1, 900	34. 0	234. 2	436
¹ 2, 000	34. 9	292. 5	358
2, 100	37. 2	314. 2	355
2, 200	39. 4	350. 9	336
2, 300	40. 2	426. 6	282
2, 400	40. 9	474. 2	259

¹ Maximum sustained speed.

Sea—Moderate.
Displacement 94,500.
Draft aft—5 feet 3 inches.
Draft forward—2 feet 5 inches.

One engine operation.

TABLE 1.—*Fuel consumption and cruising radius, one engine, Admiral, (29/30) wheels*

77-FOOT ELCO BOAT

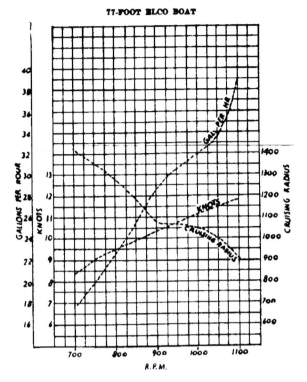

Two engine operation.

TABLE 2.—*Fuel consumption and cruising radius, two engines, Admiral, (29/30) wheels*

77-FOOT ELCO BOAT

Three engine operation.

TABLE 3.—*Fuel consumption and cruising radius, three engines, Admiral, (29/30) wheels*

77-FOOT ELCO BOAT

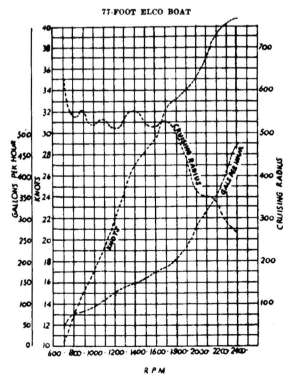

Charts showing the actual performance data of the Packard 1200 HP, V-12 gasoline marine engines. Courtesy of Elco.

Manufacturer's name plate from PT-59, well known for it's exploits at Tulagi against the Tokyo Express coming down the "Slot." Courtesy of PT Boats Museum.

13

CAMOUFLAGE

During World War II, camouflage schemes or measures were developed for each type of vessel. Measure 31, also named Dark Pattern System, was designed for offshore operations.

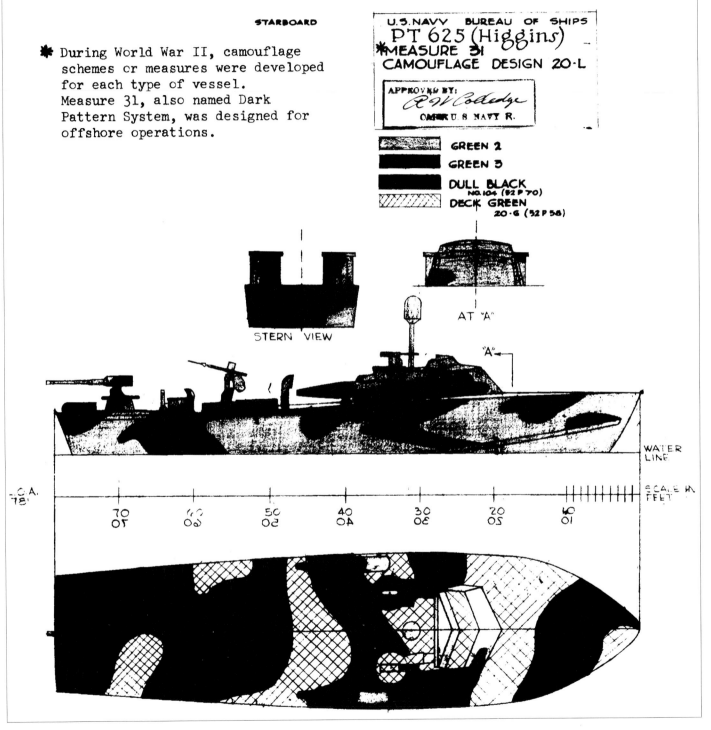

The camouflage of PT boats was used for the sole purpose of making them difficult to spot by the enemy. To standardize the camouflage schemes, the Bureau of Ships (Buships), under the direction of Captain Henry A. Ingram, issued various approved designs.

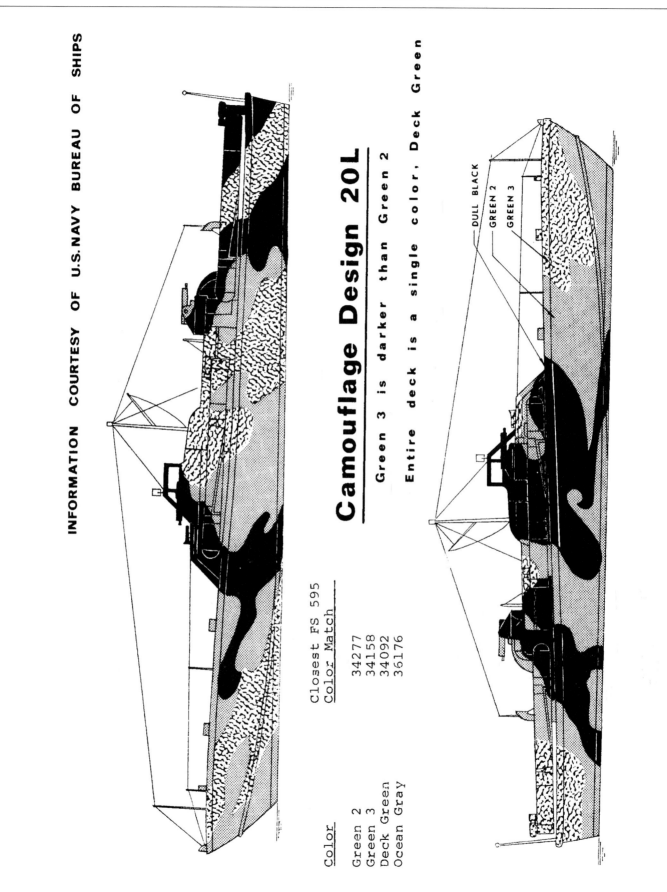

INFORMATION COURTESY OF U.S.NAVY BUREAU OF SHIPS

Camouflage Design 20L

Green 3 is darker than Green 2

Entire deck is a single color, Deck Green

DULL BLACK
GREEN 2
GREEN 3

Closest FS 595
Color Match

Color	
Green 2	34277
Green 3	34158
Deck Green	34092
Ocean Gray	36176

Courtesy of the United States Navy Bureau of Ships.

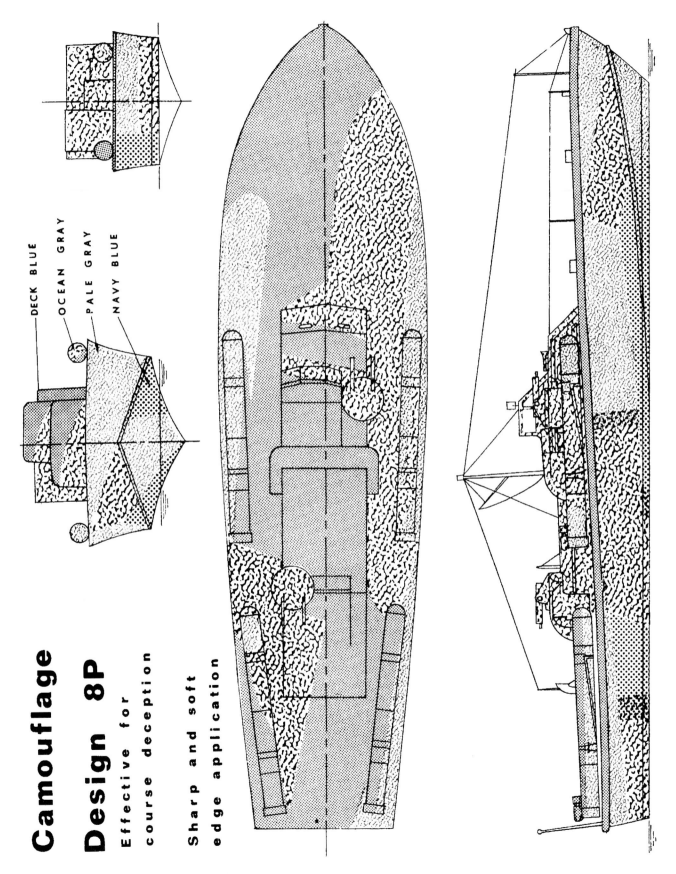

Camouflage
Design 8P

Effective for
course deception

Sharp and soft
edge application

DECK BLUE
OCEAN GRAY
PALE GRAY
NAVY BLUE

Courtesy of the United States Navy Bureau of Ships.

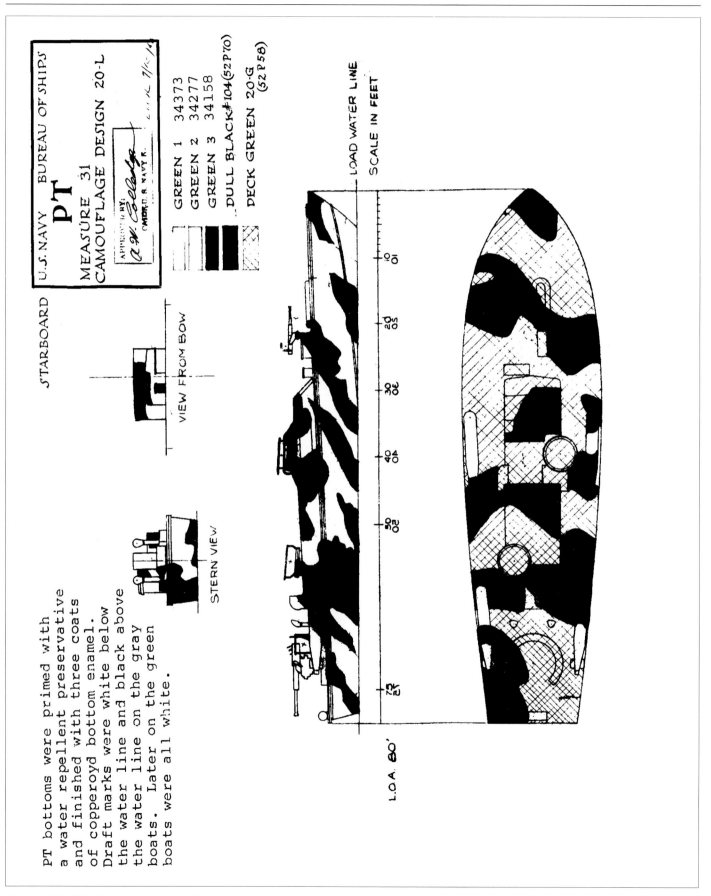

U.S. NAVY   BUREAU OF SHIPS

PT

MEASURE 31
CAMOUFLAGE DESIGN 20-L

APPROVED BY:
A.N. Colely
CMDR., U.S. NAVY, R.

STARBOARD

GREEN 1   34373
GREEN 2   34277
GREEN 3   34158
DULL BLACK #104 (52P70)
DECK GREEN 20-G (52P58)

VIEW FROM BOW

STERN VIEW

LOAD WATER LINE

SCALE IN FEET

L.O.A. 80'

PT bottoms were primed with
a water repellent preservative
and finished with three coats
of copperoyd bottom enamel.
Draft marks were white below
the water line and black above
the water line on the gray
boats. Later on the green
boats were all white.

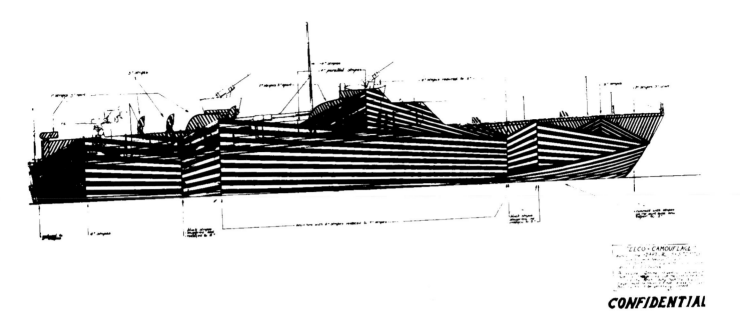

CONFIDENTIAL

Instructional copy of Elco camouflage technique based on the "Adaptor System" of Lt. Cdr. George C. Evans. Zebra stripe was used to create confusion regarding the identity of the craft and course direction. It was not successful. Courtesy of the United States Navy.

ABOVE AND NEXT PAGE: The black and white zebra type pattern created confusion and reduced visibility at ranges over a mile. However, for night and close quarters operation in the Pacific, it proved to be ineffective. The crews quickly painted over them with dark green paint to merge better with the jungle. The only area the zebra type pattern was used was in the Mediterranean theater of operation. Courtesy of the PT Boat Museum.

Here, an experiment with another kind of camouflage which even covered the new appendage at the stern of the boat. The attachment was an additional gas tank used to increase cruising range. While underway, the wake of the boat would lift the tank to reduce drag. It was designed to be dropped when empty. During the trial run, many problems surfaced and the tank broke loose during high speed sharp turns. Courtesy of the PT Boat Museum.

14

TACTICS AND FORMATIONS

Patrol and Barge Attack Doctrine

PTs normally patrol at low speed with mufflers closed, close to the beach so that no barges can pass the PT and the beach without being sighted. PTs also attempt to stay sufficiently close to shore to sight any barges that may be loading or unloading on the beach. The distances offshore vary according to conditions of visibility and known positions of reefs and shore batteries. Most barge patrols are conducted from twenty to one thousand yards offshore.

PTs patrol in an offshore echelon to lessen risk of grounding for following boats.

As soon as barges are sighted, PTs close range at high speed to fifty yards or less, opening fire at about 200 yards. The PTs, in column, make a run past the line of barges, firing with all guns that can be brought to bear. The PTs then withdraw, reform and return for another run on any barges that may have survived the first run. As many runs are made as are required for destruction of all the barges, except when the shore fire is sufficiently heavy and accurate to force the PTs to withdraw.

The essence of the attack is surprise and speed in order to close the range and sink the barges before they have time to make the beach. Where a group of unusually large barges is encountered, it is doctrine for the attacking PTs to form on line of bearings perpendicular to the bearing of barges for approach to attack, and for boats to turn into column, parallel to the barges, and open fire on order. This is to permit all boats to open fire at once and to present as many different targets as possible to the enemy, rather than to have all barges return fire concentrated on the lead boat.

The use of tracers has a lot to do with the inaccuracy of the enemy's return fire. They cannot face the hail of red balls coming their way and stay on with their own guns. However, too much tracer in our own fire tends to blind the gunners. Therefore, a compromise must be made. Preferred belting is 5 armor piercing, 3 incendiary, 2 tracer. Some discretion is permitted to individual boats in ammunition belting.

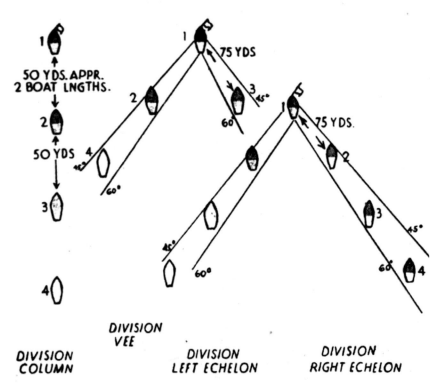

A division of PT boats was normally composed of three boats or a maximum of four. From this, all maneuvers and evolution follow. The three basic formations are division column, division V and division echelon.

Division column. Courtesy of the United States Navy.

Division V. Courtesy of the United States Navy.

Division Echelon. Courtesy of the United States Navy.

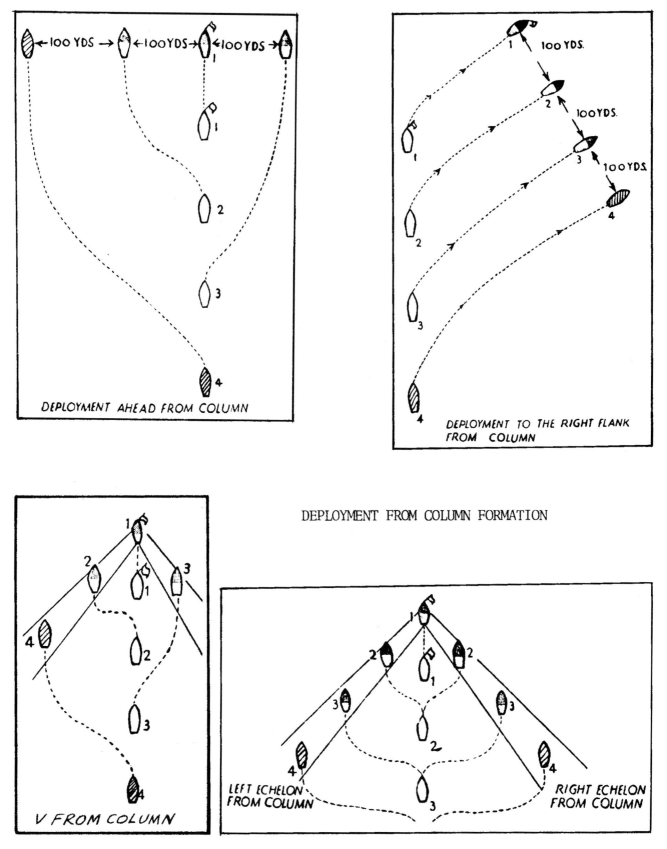

Deployment from column formation. Courtesy of the National Archives.

Division column Formation. Courtesy of the United States Navy.

Deployment to the right flank from column. Courtesy of the PT Boat Museum.

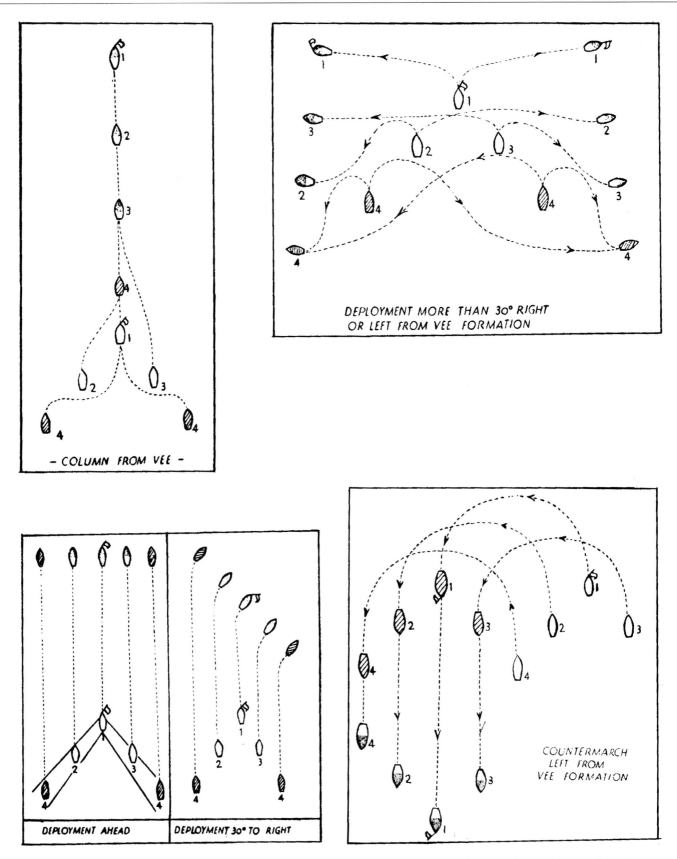

- COLUMN FROM VEE -

DEPLOYMENT MORE THAN 30° RIGHT
OR LEFT FROM VEE FORMATION

DEPLOYMENT AHEAD

DEPLOYMENT 30° TO RIGHT

COUNTERMARCH
LEFT FROM
VEE FORMATION

The V formation was most commonly used in PT boat operations. It was wide, compact, permitted rapid development and reduced chances of enfilade. It also offered an excellent defense against attacking aircraft. Courtesy of the National Archives.

Higgins boats in division V formation. Courtesy of PT Boat Museum.

Another view of Higgins boats in V formation. Courtesy of the PT Boat Museum.

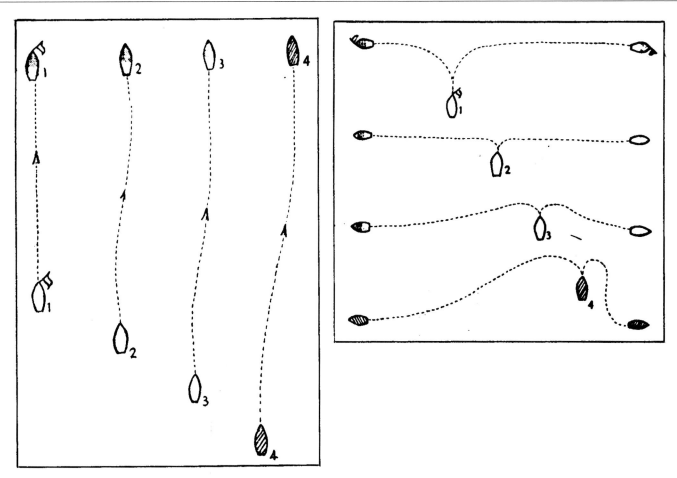

The echelon formation was normally used when cruising off shore to keep boats behind the leader from hitting a hidden reef or other obstruction. It was more unwieldy and subject to enfilade. Courtesy of the National Archives.

Two divisions of PT boats in echelon formation. Courtesy of the National Archives.

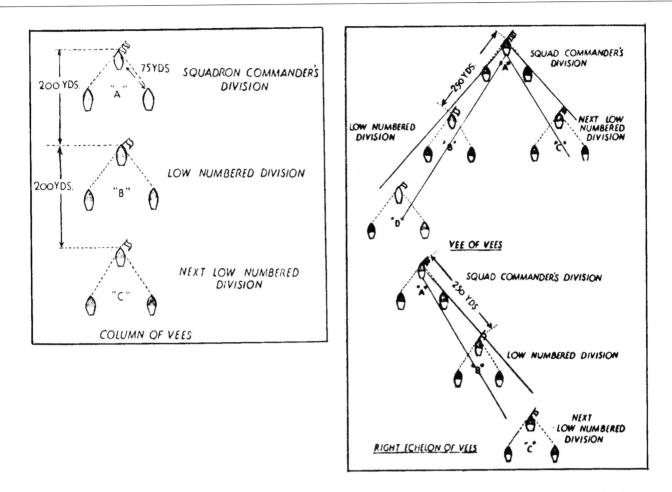

A squadron of PT boats is composed of two or more divisions. Squadron formation is used for cruising, operating with other units of the fleet, and leading to an attack position. There are three basic squadron formations: Column of V's, Vee of Vees and echelon of Vees. Courtesy of the National Archives.

Three divisions of PT boats in squadron formation column Vees. Courtesy of the United States Navy.

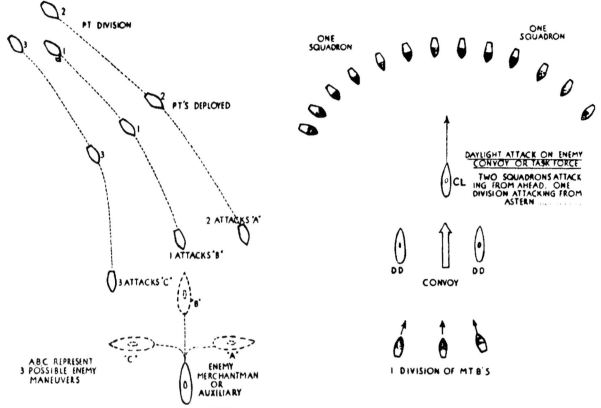

In developing an attack, the captain of the PT boat should use stealth in closing the range and seek a favorable attack course where the speed of his boat can best be used. The direction of the wind should be considered for carrying sound and laying smoke. The use of sun and moon to blind and silhouette the enemy, respectively, should be coordinated in the attack plan. In attacking unprotected transports or cargo vessels, the lead PT boat should get into torpedo range to fire its torpedoes. Other boats should follow up and fire torpedoes if necessary. The depth charges may be used to finish off a crippled vessel. In making a daylight attack on enemy convoys, the PT boats, in squadron formation, should be led to the position sharp on the bow of the convoy. The divisions should be released at this point to press home their attacks individually. Teamwork is essential in picking appropriate targets without encroaching on an adjacent boat's territory. One or more divisions may attack the convoy from behind to take advantage of the confusion from the frontal attack. Courtesy of the National Archives.

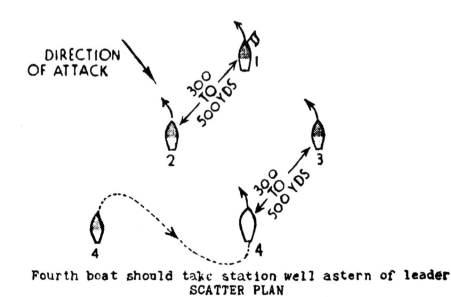

If a division of PT boats is attacked by enemy aircraft, the best defense is to disperse into the V formation to give maximum fire support to each other. When under attack by dive bomber, a boat should make a sharp turn at high speed after the bomber has started its dive. During the strafing attack by aircraft, it is better to cut across the line of fire at high speed rather than straight and risk being raked from ahead or behind. Courtesy of the National Archives.

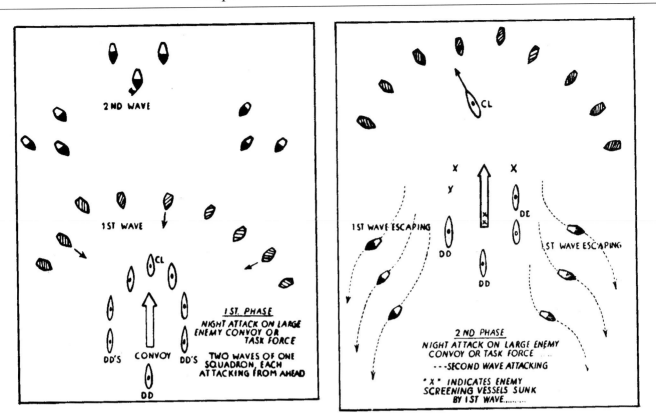

At night the attack should be carried out in two or three waves. Each subsequent wave should take advantage of the confusion caused by the previous wave. The first wave may even renew the attack after the last wave. Courtesy of the National Archives.

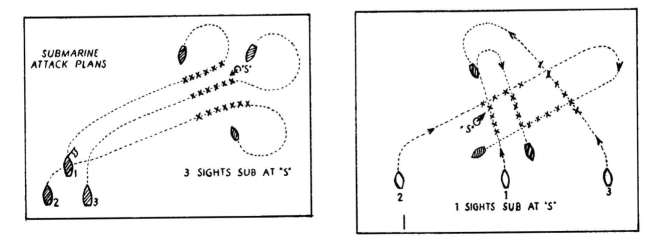

Upon sighting an enemy submarine, the boat first making contact should attack immediately and signal the other boats by gunfire or radio. The chance of destroying the submarine decreases as the square of the time between sighting and dropping depth charges. The following general attack rules apply: 1. When the range is less than 1000 yards, use 100 foot depth settings of depth charges. When greater, use 200 foot settings. 2. Best attack speed is 36 knots. 3. Slow to 20 knots when dropping depth charges. Courtesy of the National Archives.

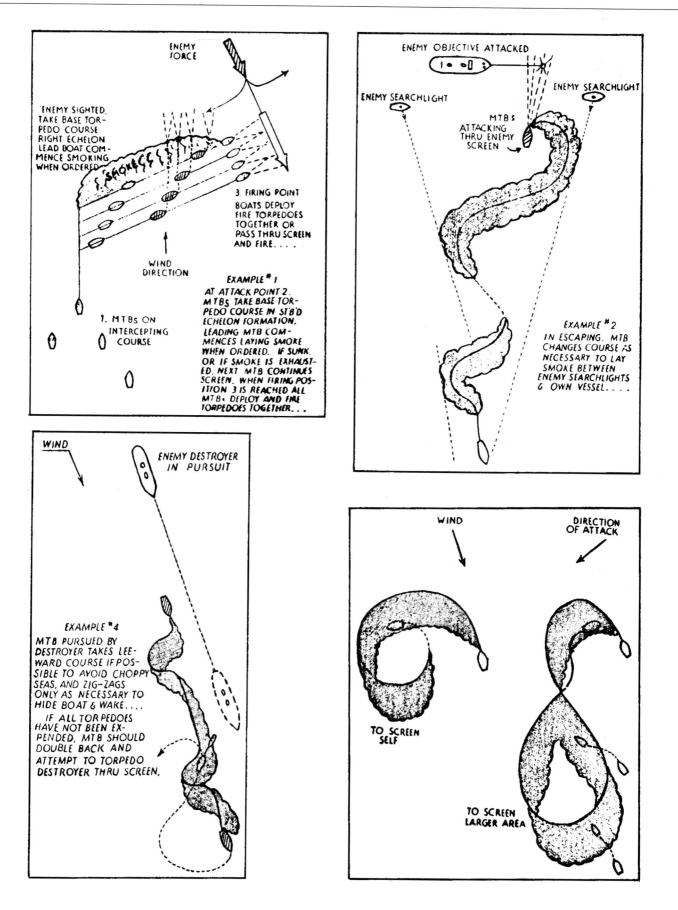

ENEMY FORCE

ENEMY SIGHTED.
TAKE BASE TOR-
PEDO COURSE
RIGHT ECHELON
LEAD BOAT COM-
MENCE SMOKING
WHEN ORDERED

SMOKE

3. FIRING POINT
BOATS DEPLOY
FIRE TORPEDOES
TOGETHER OR
PASS THRU SCREEN
AND FIRE.....

WIND
DIRECTION

1. MTBs ON
INTERCEPTING
COURSE

EXAMPLE #1
AT ATTACK POINT 2.
MTBS TAKE BASE TOR-
PEDO COURSE IN ST'B'D
ECHELON FORMATION.
LEADING MTB COM-
MENCES LAYING SMOKE
WHEN ORDERED. IF SUNK
OR IF SMOKE IS EXHAUST-
ED, NEXT MTB CONTINUES
SCREEN. WHEN FIRING POS-
ITION 3 IS REACHED ALL
MTB's DEPLOY AND FIRE
TORPEDOES TOGETHER...

ENEMY OBJECTIVE ATTACKED

ENEMY SEARCHLIGHT

ENEMY SEARCHLIGHT

MTBs
ATTACKING
THRU ENEMY
SCREEN

EXAMPLE #2
IN ESCAPING. MTB
CHANGES COURSE AS
NECESSARY TO LAY
SMOKE BETWEEN
ENEMY SEARCHLIGHTS
& OWN VESSEL.....

WIND

ENEMY DESTROYER
IN PURSUIT

EXAMPLE #4
MTB PURSUED BY
DESTROYER TAKES LEE-
WARD COURSE IF POS-
SIBLE TO AVOID CHOPPY
SEAS, AND ZIG-ZAGS
ONLY AS NECESSARY TO
HIDE BOAT & WAKE.....
IF ALL TORPEDOES
HAVE NOT BEEN EX-
PENDED, MTB SHOULD
DOUBLE BACK AND
ATTEMPT TO TORPEDO
DESTROYER THRU SCREEN.

WIND

DIRECTION
OF ATTACK

TO SCREEN
SELF

TO SCREEN
LARGER AREA

A PT boat using smoke to protect landing craft during an amphibious landing. Courtesy of the PT Boat Museum.

OPPOSITE: Smoke screen is used by PT boats under the following conditions: 1. In making a long range daylight attack on enemy vessel and in retiring from such attack. 2. In escaping after an attack, when illuminated by enemy's searchlight. 3. As a protection against enemy aircraft or pursuing vessels, and screening an amphibious landing. One tank of smoke normally carried aboard a PT boat is estimated to be capable of laying a screen for about three miles at maximum speed. Courtesy of the National Archives.

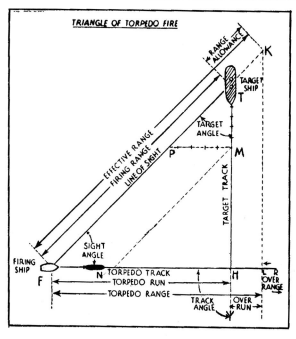

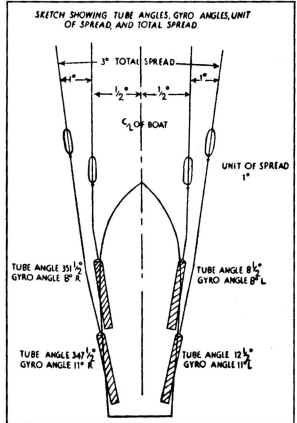

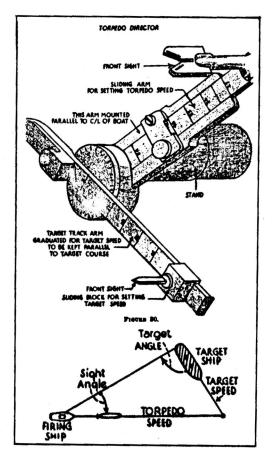

The purpose of a torpedo control is to direct the torpedoes to produce a maximum number of hits on target. Basically it is just a matter of aiming the boat in the direction of a collision course with the moving target. To understand torpedo control it is important to know that torpedo tubes, mounted on deck, must be swung out a small amount to permit the torpedoes to clear the deck. In order for the torpedoes to straighten out and run parallel to the boat after launching, gyro angles are pre-set on the torpedoes before they are placed in the tubes. To help aim the PT boat, the torpedo director is used. This unit is mounted on the bridge with the torpedo track arm parallel to the center line of the boat. An even simpler device used in torpedo control is the Mark 7 portable angle solver, commonly known as an "izwas." It consisted of a number of discs and a celluloid runner. By setting up the estimated target angle and target speed, the sight angle can be obtained. By adding the sight angle to present target bearing, the torpedo firing course can be obtained. Torpedoes can be fired electronically from the bridge or by emergency percussion with a mallet by a torpedoman stationed at the tubes. It is standard practice to retard throttles at the moment of firing to allow the torpedoes to clear before changing course. It is also desirable to have the boat on a steady keel (horizontal) with the tubes as horizontal as possible at the moment of firing. Courtesy of the National Archives.

A Torpedoman standing by with a mallet ready to strike the emergency percussion. Courtesy of the PT Boat Museum.

GENERAL QUARTERS

During patrol or on a mission when an encounter with the enemy is highly probable, fully ready condition is assumed with the crew at general quarters. Fully ready condition, sometimes called Condition I, means:

1. Electric power.
    a. Electric power up to the firing switches of all firing circuits.
2. Bridge control equipment.
    a. Steering control shifted to outside station.
    b. Torpedo director uncovered.
    c. Telescope cover removed.
3. Tubes.
    a. Tubes trained out and secured in that position.
    b. Firing circuits ready for firing.
    c. Loaded and primed impulse cartridges in impulse chambers.
    d. Firing mechanisms set for local percussion as well as electric firing.
4. Torpedoes.
    a. Fully ready for the run.
    b. Depth setting made for the type of target most likely to be encountered.
    c. Torpedo speed set for the highest available.
    d. Gyro angles set as required.
    e. Unit of spread set for 1 degree.

GENERAL QUARTERS! Courtesy of the National Archives.

5. 20 mm gun.

    a. Gun cocked. (should be uncocked for a few minutes every four hours)

    b. If weather is wet, cover over magazine and breech mechanism, not over muzzle.

    c. Safety on until ready to commence firing.

    d. Magazine in place.

    e. If weather permits, gun is manned continuously. If not, gun secured pointing up.

6. Machine guns.

    a. Covers removed.

    b. Ammo belt up to gun, loaded and put on safety until ready to fire.

    c. If weather is wet, keep muzzle bags on guns, cover over turret.

    d. Gun manned, trained on bow or probable target bearing.

Commander William C. Specht (at left) on the bridge of an Elco 77 foot boat. He organized the Motor Torpedo Boat Squadrons Training Center at Melville, Rhode Island. The Center came to be known as "Specht Tech" and began operations in the middle of March 1942. All subsequent tactics and doctrines used in combat were developed at the center. Courtesy of the PT Boat Museum.

The Motor Torpedo Boat Training Center at Melville, Rhode Island where all PT crews received their training. Courtesy of the United States Navy.

7. Depth Charges.

    a. Replace plain safety caps with knobbed safety caps secured to racks. Do not wire safety forks to racks.

    b. Depth settings are set as directed by the boat captain.

8. Personnel Duties.

    a. Captain - wheel or throttle

    b. Executive officer - Throttle or wheel

    c. Gunner's mate - 20 mm gun.

    d. Torpedo man - Stand by torpedoes or depth charges.

    e. Quartermaster - Ammunition passer for .50 caliber machine guns.

    f. Radioman - Radio

    g. Machinist's mate - Engine room.

    h. machine gunner's mate - .50 caliber machine guns.

PT 552 underway with crew at general quarters. Courtesy of the PT Boat Museum.

PT BOAT BUILDING PROGRAM

1 and 2 - Fogal Boat Yard, Inc.
3 and 4 - Fisher Boat Works
5 and 6 - Higgins
7 and 8 - Philadelphia Navy Yard
9 - British Power Boat Company (Purchased by Elco)
10 through 69 - Elco 70 foot.
20 through 68 - Elco 77 foot
69 - Huckins experimental boat
70 - Higgins (Dream Boat)
71 through 94 - Higgins
95 through 102 - Huckins
103 through 196 - Elco 80 foot
197 through 254 - Higgins
255 through 264 - Huckins
265 through 313 - Higgins
314 through 361 - Elco
362 through 367 - Harbor (Elco model built at West Coast)

368 through 371 - Canadian Power Boat Company
372 through 383 - Elco
384 through 399 - Jacobs (Vosper boats for Lend-Lease)
400 through 429 - Annapolis (Vosper boats for Lend-Lease)
430 through 449 - Herreschoff (Vosper boats for Lend-Lease)
450 through 485 - Higgins
486 through 563 - Elco
564 - Higgins (Experimental Hellcat 70 foot boat)
565 through 622 - Elco
623 through 624 - Elco (Contract canceled)
625 through 660 - Higgins (Lend-Lease to USSR)
661 through 730 - Annapolis (Vosper boats for Lend-Lease)
731 through 760 - Elco (Shipped to USSR)
761 through 790 - Elco (Contract canceled)
791 through 796 - Higgins
797 through 808 - Higgins (Contract canceled, eventually sold to Argentine Navy)

PT boats, Elco and Fisher, tie up at dock at MTB Squadron Training Center at Melville, Rhode Island. Note first PT tender, USS NIAGARA, a converted Yacht. Courtesy of the PT Boat Museum.

Aerial view of the Elco plant in Bayonne, N.J. where 398 PT boats were produced during World War II. Courtesy of Elco.

PT 564 - Higgins experimental HELLCAT used for design research only. Courtesy of the National Archives.

The Steuben crystal sculpture "VOYAGE" was presented to President John F. Kennedy on March 14, 1962 by the Peter Tare Organization. The piece, symbolizing the passage of time from war service to the Presidency, was designed by Mr. Donald Pollard. Courtesy of Steuben Glass.

Lt. Commander John D. Bulkeley, the father of PT boats. As lieutenant, he assumed command of Squadron 3 stationed in the Philippines. He evacuated General Douglas MacArthur on board PT 41 and received the Medal of Honor from President Franklin D. Roosevelt. Courtesy of the Warner Research Center.

Five decades after World War II, there are only 18 PT boats left in this country. While there is always hope that there are more PT's out there, we only have information on these. *Courtesy of the PT Boat Museum.*

1. PT 617 (80 foot Elco) is located at Battleship Cove, Fall River, Massachusetts in static display.

2. PT 796 (78 foot Higgins) is located at Battleship Cove, Fall River, Massachusetts in static display.

3. PT 658 (78 foot Higgins) is being restored in Oregon by Save the PT boats, Incorporated.

4. PT 659 (78 foot Higgins) is being used to restore PT 658. The shell will go on static display with another museum.

5. PT 695 (71 foot Annapolis) was restored by the American Patrol Boat Association. The boat was called "PT Joe" and belonged to the late judge Joseph Marchetti.

6. PT 309 (78 foot Higgins) is located at Admiral Nimitz Museum. They intend to run her for a time and then make her a static display in Fredricksburg.

7. PT 657 (78 foot Higgins) is a big cruise boat called "Malahini" in San Diego, California.

8. PT 761 (80 foot Elco) listed as a riverboat cruiser in Jacksonville.

9. PT 615 (80 foot Elco) is called "Tar Baby" in Philadelphia.

10. PT 314 (80 foot Elco) is being restored by Roger Radbill.

11. PT 728 (71 foot Annapolis) is at Key West in Elco military configuration. Bill Bohmfalk, (305) 296-8989.

12. PT 486 (80 foot Elco) was rebuilt as "Sightseer" for daily sightseeing tour at Wildwood, New Jersey, (609) 522-2919.

13. PT 724 (71 foot Annapolis) is known as "Endeavor II."

14. PT 3 (Fisher Boat Works) is located in Philadelphia.

15. PT 8 (Philadelphia Navy Yard) is in Bayview, Texas.

16. PT 457 (78 foot Higgins) is named "Falcon" and reduced to 62 feet and 9 inches at Highlands, New Jersey.

17. PT 305 (78 foot Higgins) was cut to 60 feet and used as an oyster boat at Tilgman, Maryland.

18. PT 459 (78 foot Higgins) was cut to 65 feet for Fire Island Charter & Ferry boat.

15

LAST MODEL

Courtesy of the PT Boat Museum.

Bow view of PT 596. Courtesy of the PT Boat Museum.

PT 596, Squadron 40, placed in service May 10, 1945. Assigned to the Pacific Fleet. It served at Samar, Philippines but saw no action. Courtesy of the PT Boat Museum.

16

EXPORT

In March 1941, 73 foot boats (PT 10 through PT 19 and PT 9) were transferred to the Royal Navy as MTB 258 through MTB 268. PT 9 was allocated to the Royal Canadian Navy. The other ten boats were modified to the Royal Navy's specifications. The modification included replacing the four trainable 18 inch torpedo tubes with two 21 inch fixed tubes. The domes covering the two turrets were removed and a 20 mm Oerlikon gun was installed at the stern. Depth charge track was added on both sides of the boat. The boats arrived at Alexandria and formed into the 10th MTB Flotilla under the command of LCDR Noakes.

PT 49 through PT 58 (77 foot boats) were also transferred to the Royal Navy as MTB 307 through MTB 316. The four torpedo tubes were replaced with two 21 inch tubes. The twin turrets were replaced with a single Vickers Mark V turret on the centerline of the coachroof. The 20 mm gun at the stern was retained. Depth charge track was installed on either side of the boat. These boats were formed into the 15th MTB Flotilla.

Test firing the twin .30 cal. Lewis machine guns on board MTB 263. Courtesy of the PT Boat Museum.

H.M.S. MTB 263 (XPT 14). Armament consists of two 21 foot torpedo tubes (British built), two depth charges, one 20 mm Oerlikon gun, two twin, .50 cal Elco Dewandre turrets and two twin .30 Lewis machine gun mounts. Courtesy of the PT Boat Museum.

MTB 263 undergoing trials by Elco in November, 1941. Courtesy of the PT Boat Museum.

21 foot British LC MK 1 Torpedo tube on Elco foundations. Courtesy of the PT Boat Museum.

Test firing all guns on board MTB 263. Note Dewandre turrets with twin .50 caliber machine guns. Courtesy of the PT Boat Museum.

More than 100 71 foot Vosper boats were built by Jacob (PT 384-399), Annapolis (PT 430-449) and Herreschoff (PT 430-449) in the United States for England and the USSR under Land-lease. Courtesy of the Warner Research Center.

17

POST WAR PERIOD

In 1945 the Navy authorized the construction of four new experimental PT boats incorporating lessons learned in four years of combat. Although each of the four boats had different characteristics, they all had aluminum hulls and were powered by four 2500 hp Packard engines. They were:

PT 809, Electric Boat Company, August 7, 1950.

PT 810, Bath Iron Works Corporation, June 2, 1950.

PT 811, John Trumphy & Sons, November 30. 1950.

PT 812, Philadelphia Naval Shipyard, February 1, 1951.

Their common specifications were:

Power-(4) 16 cylinder V type W-100 IM3300 Packard Marine engine, 2500 hp at 2700 rpm each, high octane gasoline.

Armament-(2) 40 mm air cooled guns with optical sights. (2) 20 mm Oerlikon dual guns with optical sights. (1) 81 mm mortar in traverse mount. (4) Racks for 21 inch torpedoes. (1) Smoke generator.

Navigation - AN-SPS-5 radar, MK 18, model 4, gyrocompass and Bendix autopilot.

Insignia of Motor Torpedo Boat Squadron 1 (Post War). Courtesy of James B. Stewart.

Their individual specifications were:

	PT 809	PT 810	PT 811	PT 812
Displacement (tons)	94.5	89.5	90	102
Length	98' 6"	89' 5 1/4"	94' 11"	105'
Beam	26' 6"	24' 1"	24' 11"	22' 5 1/2"
Draft (maximum)	5' 6"	5' 10"	4' 2"	5' 5"
Fuel Capacity (gallons)	6960	7014	6960	6790
Number of propellers	4	4	4	4
Rudders	4	2	4	4
Hull section form	Concave V	Convex V	Ogee V	Round

These boats had completed the builders' sea trials and were delivered to Motor Torpedo Squadron 1 in the summer of 1951. From that time until 1956, Motor Torpedo Squadron 1 performed operational development and testing of these four boats at Norfolk.

During the trials the following findings were disclosed: 1. PT 809 proved rough riding in seaway. 2. PT 810's deck and cabin arrangement were inefficient. 3. PT 811 proved to be the fastest boat in calm water (55 knots) and had the best deck and cabin layout. 4. PT 812 was the slowest boat in calm water but fastest in state III sea and also the most seaworthy. Her low silhouette was

praised, but deck access was poor. 5. All boats had trouble starting when their engines were hot. 6. The torpedoes were too slow and the boats often caught up and ran over them during high speed launching.

In 1957, PT 812 was converted to use gas turbines which marked the first time a turbine engine was used in small craft in this country. After conversion, she had two 12 cylinder 60 degree V 600 hp Packard ID-1700-T4 marine diesels with reversible pitch propellers for maneuvering and two open cycle 4000 hp Metropolitan Vickers gas turbines for main propulsion.

PT 809 off Norfolk, Virginia. Courtesy of the United States Navy.

PT 810 makes a high speed run with the its crew at General Quarters in Chesapeake Bay. Courtesy of the United States Navy.

PT 811 on a high speed run in the Chesapeake Bay. Courtesy of the United States Navy.

Motor Torpedo Boat Squadron 1 was decommissioned in 1959 after completion of sea trials to test the performance of the four boats. PT 809 was renamed GUARDIAN and is used by the Secret Service as a guard boat for the SEQUOIA, a yacht used by the President and other officials of the Department of Defense. She is unarmed and her superstructure was modified to suit her new role. PT 810 and PT 811 were struck from the Naval Register in 1960 but reinstated in December 1962 as PTF 1 and 2. After a shakedown cruise at Norfolk, Virginia, in June 1963, they left for Subic Bay in the Philippines and were eventually assigned to SEAL teams in Vietnam. In August, 1965 they were struck again and sunk as target. PT 812 was struck in 1960 and was transferred to Korea in April, 1967 after removal of her gas turbines. She was ultimately scrapped in 1968.

PT 812 going through a sea trial. Courtesy of James B. Stewart.

PT 812 after conversion. Courtesy of James B. Stewart.

18

MODELS

Precision model of PT 661, Vosper type, built for Bureau of Ships. Courtesy of the Bureau of Ships.

Beautiful model of PT 21, Elco 77 footer, as displayed in Cabrillo Beach Marine Museum, San Pedro, California. Model was built by Mr. Mark H. Davis. Courtesy of Mark H. Davis.

This Varney model kit of a PT boat came out during World War II. It was the first PT boat kit and was made out of wood. This model was built by David Pappmeier recently and dedicated to the crew of PT 123. Courtesy of the PT Boat Museum.

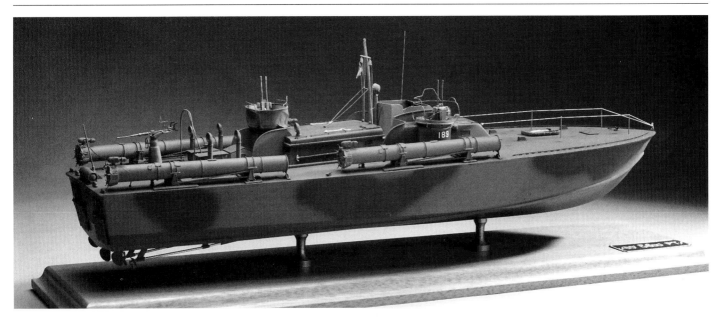

This kit (by Blue Jacket, P.O. Box 425, Stockton, Maine 04981) includes a pre-carved basswood hull shaped wood deckhouse, strip wood and styrene, brass and aluminum tubing, brass rod and over 200 specially made Britannia metal and photo-etched brass parts. Overall model length 23 1/2 inches, scale 1/16 inch to 1 foot. The kit was researched and developed by Al Ross. Courtesy of Blue Jacket.

Pictures of 1:20 scale PT boat model (built by Fine Art Models, P.O. Box 225, Birmingham, MI 48012) in two different paint schemes. The detail on this model is made of hand fabricated brass, from the 37 mm and 20 mm cannons to the four 50 caliber machine guns. Courtesy of Fine Art Models.

This model was on loan from the Navy to President John F. Kennedy and was on display in his office at the time of his assassination. Although 109 was painted on, this model depicts a much later type PT boat than the one Lt. Kennedy was on. Courtesy of the Navel Ship Research and Development Center.

This model of PT 155 was built by William B. Smallshaw from a Revell kit. Courtesy of William B. Smallshaw.

PT 596 (Howard Enterprises, 24734 Winlock Drive, Torrance, CA 90505) is a conversion kit for the Dumas PT 109 kit (1/20th scale). Everything shown in the picture is included in the kit along with a 24 page instruction booklet and 85 minutes video tape demonstrating the conversion procedure. Courtesy of Howard Enterprises.

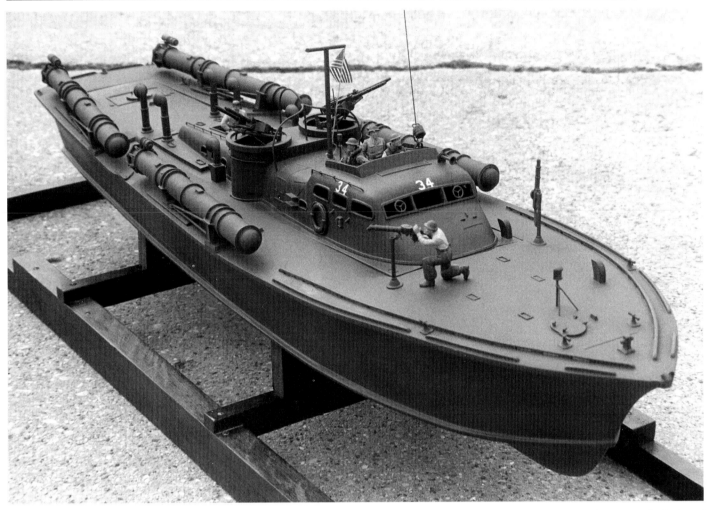

Model Elco 77 footer, PT 34, 1/24 scale, by Wayne Traxel. Hull is planked with two layers of balsa coated with five coats of polyester resin. Deck is two wooden laminated layers of 3/32" balsa followed by 1/6 basswood. Superstructure framing and planking is two laminated layers of 1/32" balsa, sealed with three coats of polyester resin. Courtesy of Wayne Traxel.

*This model was presented to President John F. Kennedy by the Washington International Boat and Sport Show in December 1962. It is now on display at John F. Kennedy Library, Columbia Point, Boston, Massachusetts 02125.*Courtesy of the John f. Kennedy Library.

APPENDIX I

Source: Higgins Industries, Inc.

Motor Torpedo Boat Seamanship

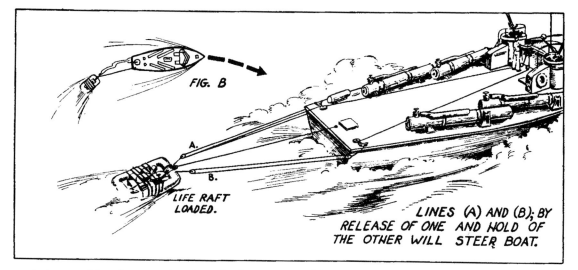

FIG. B

LIFE RAFT LOADED.

LINES (A) AND (B); BY RELEASE OF ONE AND HOLD OF THE OTHER WILL STEER BOAT.

A jury rudder for a motor torpedo boat with a damaged rudder is shown above, utilizing a life raft loaded and towed aft. The towing line is fastened to the center of the transom. Transom is then rove between the life raft and the quarters to the steering wheel. This jury rig is easier to assemble than the jury rig utilizing the locker door, but is not as satisfactory in heavy weather as the door and boat hook rig.

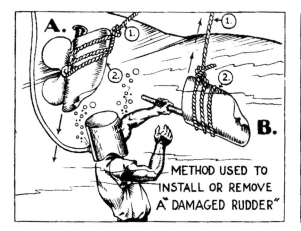

METHOD USED TO INSTALL OR REMOVE A "DAMAGED RUDDER"

EMERGENCY TILLER

IMPROVISED WHEEL STEERING TO TILLER.

Method of removing a damaged rudder. The same method can be used for re-installing a new or repaired rudder. Some naval combat motor boat operators have learned to use a gas mask and an air pump on underwater repairs.

This drawing shows an improvised rig between a motor torpedo boat steering wheel and the emergency tiller. It is an easier and more convenient rig than steering with the emergency tiller alone.

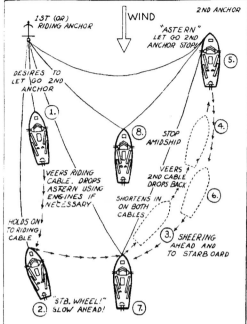

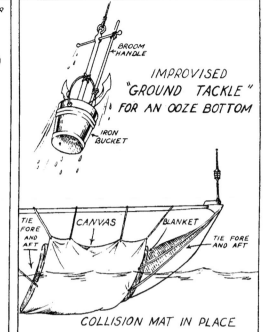

Left—Sketch showing the various steps in putting out two anchors. Postion (1) shows a motor torpedo boat riding to one anchor when the skipper decides that the second anchor is necessary. In position (2) after releasing more cable the starboard wheel is revolving ahead slowly. The boat steers to starboard as in position (3) to (4) and thence to (5), when abeam of the first anchor the second is let go. The motor torpedo boat is then dropped back to (6), and finally to position (7), where both anchor cables are shortened to position (8), the final riding position of the motor torpedo boat. Riding to two anchors is necessary in small coves where a lack of sea room prevents riding out the storm to a long anchor line. The anchor cable should be from five to seven times the depth of the water when the single anchor is used. Where sea room permits, it is better to use two anchors 30 to 40 yards apart on a single anchor line. During storms, anchor lines of rope must be watched every

Right—Lower drawing shows an emergency repair to a damaged boat hull. A tarpaulin is lashed to the boat's side by means of rope ties fore and aft, with a blanket as a padding between the hull and the canvas. Pillows can be jammed into the hole from inside the boat. Emergency repairs of this kind will keep a boat afloat and enable the crew to reach a marine railway where permanent repairs can be made. The upper drawing shows the boat hook and bucket used in connection with the conventional type of kedge anchor on an oozy bottom, where the anchor alone will not hold. A broom handle may be used instead of a boat hook. This improvised ground tackle will hold a boat in the sofetest bottom during the hardest blow.

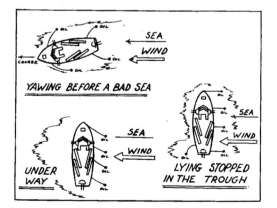

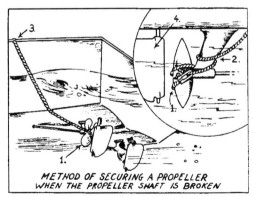

Left—The sketch in the upper left-hand corner shows the use of oil bags to prevent yawing before a bad following sea. The lower drawings show the use of oil bags, both when underway and when stopped in the trough of a heavy sea.

Sometimes when the propeller of a motor torpedo boat strikes a rock or a shallow spot, not only is the rudder damaged, but frequently the shaft is broken. The shaft slips along the shaft alley until the weight of the propeller holds the shaft against the upper part of the strut bearing. On some occasions the shaft and the propeller are entirely lost, causing water to flow into the engine room through the shaft tunnel. The above sketch shows a method of securing the propeller and shaft by lashing, preventing such a loss as the boat returns to port for repairs under power from the opposite motor.

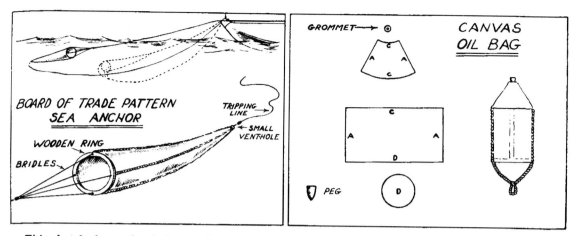

This sketch shows the design of the British Board of Trade pattern sea anchor. It is long and narrow and has a small vent-hole at the small end of the cone and a wooden ring. The upper sketch shows the bow of the boat riding to such a sea anchor. The dotted line shows the same sea anchor being hauled inboard by the trip line. Sea anchors are very useful on any small boat in bad weather and should always be carried as standard equipment.

This drawing shows how a canvas oil bag is made. A grommet is inserted in the bottom of the cone of the bag. A wooden peg is used as a stopper. The peg is sent out before the oil bag is put overboard. An easier form would be a simple bag with holes punched in the bag with a needle, the bag filled with oakum and then filled with oil. The oakum or waste holds the oil and it is released through the punched holes in the bag. A little oil goes a long way.

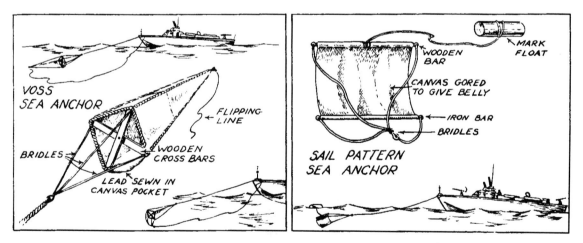

Left—The above sketch shows the Voss sea anchor, invented by Captain Voss, who sailed around the world in a 36-ft. canoe. He frequently met with bad weather, and when he did he never attempted to fight the storm but would lay to his sea anchor. To make the anchor easier to store, Voss used no wood or iron ring in the opening, such as used by American and British sea anchors. He used two crossed sticks to hold the mouth open. Wherever possible, the large end of a sea anchor should have a diameter of 1 inch for every foot of length of motor torpedo boat. This would take a 6-ft. opening for a 70-ft.

Right—An improvised sea anchor made from a square anchor with a wooden rod at the top and an iron rod at the bottom. This is another type that is popular because of its ability to be easily stored. The iron rod should be heavy enough to submerge the sea anchor.

motor torpedo boat. A 6-ft. metal ring would be a difficult article to store away. Higgins craft use a sea anchor with the ring hinged, enabling the anchor with a 6-ft. mouth to be stored in a 3-ft. space.

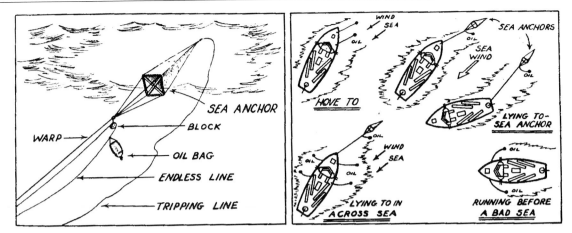

Left—When a sea anchor is used, there should be a trip extending from the tip of the sea anchor to the stern of the motor torpedo boat. Whenever it is necessary to pull in the sea anchor, a yank on the trip line reverses the sea anchor, and towed by the small end of the cone, the anchor offers no further resistance. A light tackle for sending out an oil bag should be attached to the point where the warp is belayed to the sea anchor.

Right—The above sketch shows the use of oil bags, alone or combined with sea anchors.

The upper left-hand corner shows a motor boat hove to with the wind and sea on the starboard bow, and two oil bags over the starboard bow, making an oil slick around the boat.

In the upper right-hand corner is a motor boat lying to sea anchor, first from the bow, and second from the stern. Some boats, especially those with a light freeboard forward, will not lay comfortably from the bow, but will lay with comfort from the stern.

The lower left hand corner shows the situation with a crossed sea and oil bags on both sides.

The lower right-hand corner shows a motor boat running from a bad sea with oil bags from the bow.

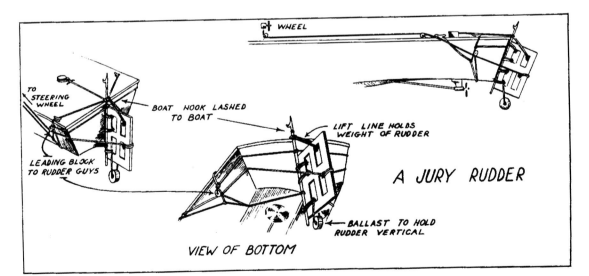

How a jury rudder can be rigged on a motor torpedo boat after the boat rudder has been damaged or shot away in action. A few yards of rope, a locker door, a boat hook and a heavy weight are the implements necessary. The locker door is lashed to the boat hook by punching three holes in the upper and lower panels. Lashed to the hole in the bottom panel is a heavy weight, such as a discarded cylinder head. The boat hook is lashed to the stern of the motor torpedo boat top and bottom. The hole above the door knob is knocked through the panel and the steering line is attached to the door at this point. The steering lines are brought through blocks to the steering wheel on deck.

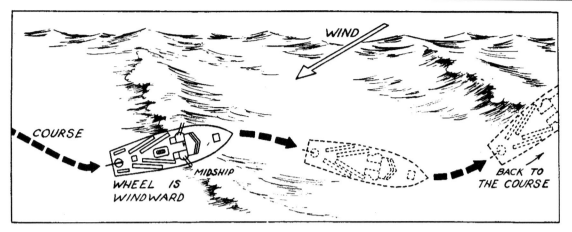

Method of "tacking" by motor boat in heavy seas. The desired course is north. The wind is blowing out of the northwest and heavy seas are running. To meet the crest of on-coming seas, the motor boat must temporarily head west northwest, returning to the original north course as soon as the crest of the sea has passed on.

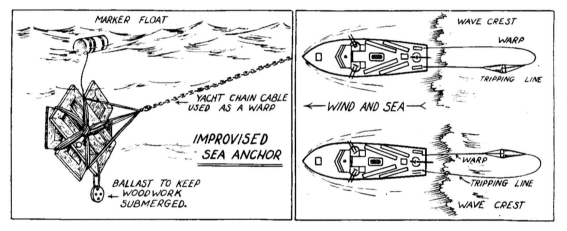

Left—In a bad storm or a hurricane a motor torpedo boat would be better off to lay to a sea anchor than to attempt to keep under way. Motor torpedo boat engines are designed for high speed. If no sea anchor is on board, one may be improvised by the use of locker panels and floor boards lashed in the form of a circular design. Then a hole may be knocked through the lower panel of a door, and a heavy weight, such as a discarded cylinder head, attached which will act as ballast to keep the woodwork submerged. A marker float, such as an empty cask, water breaker, ring buoy, or life preserver, should be attached to the upper part of this improvised sea anchor to indicate its location.

Right—Sometimes it is necessary for a motor torpedo boat to enter a small shallow inlet in bad weather when the seas are breaking all across the bar. The great danger of such a passage is that when the motor torpedo boat is on the crest of a breaking sea, it is pivoted amidships with its rudders and propellers out of the water. Under such circumstances, the helmsman has not control over the boat. There is a possibility that the boat might fall off the crest into the trough of the sea, being knocked on her beam's end and broached to. In some cases, where the seas are exceptionally high and the water very shallow in the trough, the bow might strike the bottom and the breaking sea toss the boat over end for end. This is known as "pitch poling." It has happened to several Coast Guard motor boats in the treacherous waters of our northwest coast. Under such adverse conditions, the only safe means of entering such an inlet is by the aid of a sea anchor towed aft. The upper sketch shows a motor torpedo boat entering an inlet, towing a sea anchor by a trip line. In this position there is no resistance from the sea anchor. As the crest of a large breaking wave comes up under the stern of the motor boat, the trip line is released. The sea anchor assumes the position shown in the bottom sketch. As the sea anchor fills with water, it holds the stem to right angles to the breaking sea, preventing the boat from broaching to. After the breaking sea and the danger has passed, the trip line is hauled in. The boat is again in the position of the upper sketch, the speed is increased, and the journey continued.

Right—A little oil on troubled waters will work wonders. The above four illustrations show the various uses of oil bags in bad weather. In the upper left-hand corner the drawing shows the use of oil bags when a motor torpedo boat is under way on a course at right angles to sea and wind. The upper right-hand corner shows the use of oil bags when a motor torpedo boat is stopped and is laying in the trough of the sea. The lower left-hand corner shows the use of an oil bag when a motor torpedo boat is laying with a single anchor out. A small hand tackle is attached to the anchor cable near the anchor. The oil bag is run out on this tackle. It can be brought back on board for refueling. The lower right-hand picture shows the use of oil on troubled waters when one motor torpedo boat is towing another.

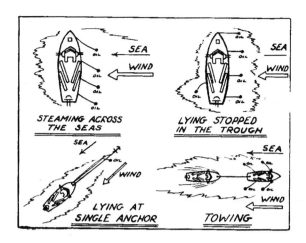

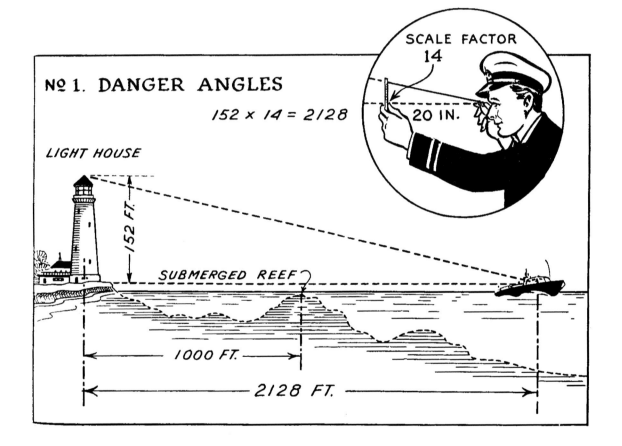

To Find Distance Multiply Height of Object By Scale Factor. Example: Height of Lighthouse 152 ft. Scale Factor 14. 152×14=2128 ft. or 709 Yards

USE STRING 20 INCHES LONG

HIGGINS INDUSTRIES INC. — New Orleans, La.

World's Largest Builders of Commercial Motorboats

RANGE FINDER

APPENDIX II

The following drawings were printed from microfilms of the original Elco drawings. Due to a fire at the Elco plant at Bayonne, N.J., in the 60's, all the records and drawings on PT boats were destroyed. Nevertheless, these drawings reflect clearly the thousands of man-hours the engineers and designers spent in producing them. Of course without these drawings, not a single PT boat can be built.

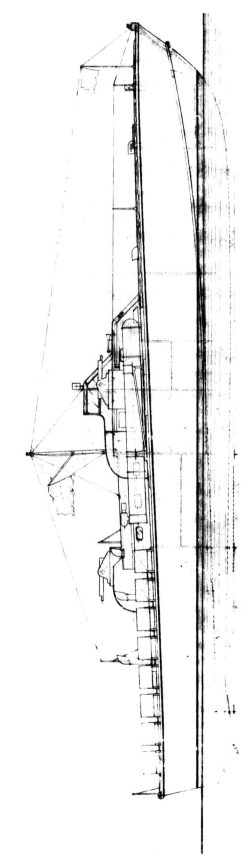

Note 0.5 inch Vickers machine guns on twin Mark V mounting and depth charges on board this boat.

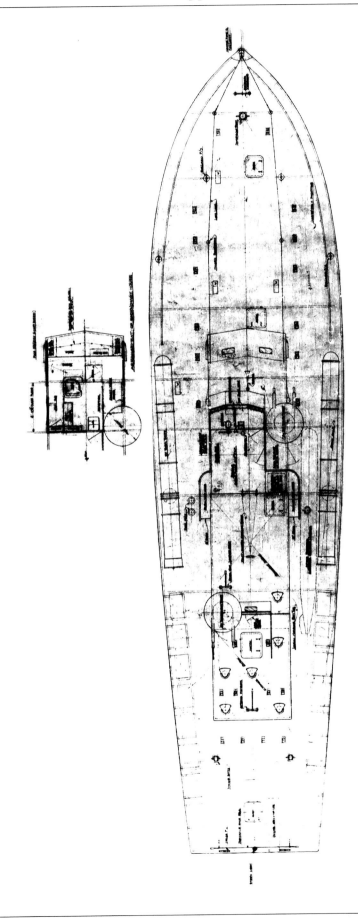

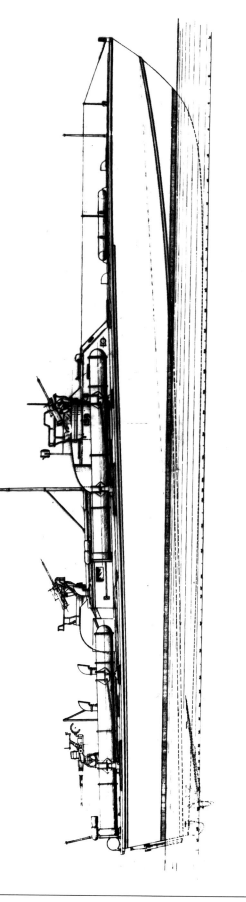

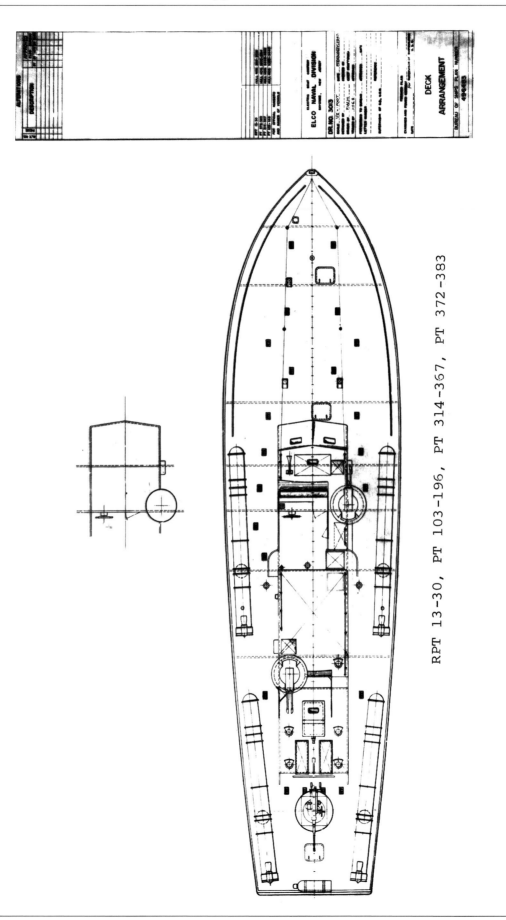

RPT 13-30, PT 103-196, PT 314-367, PT 372-383

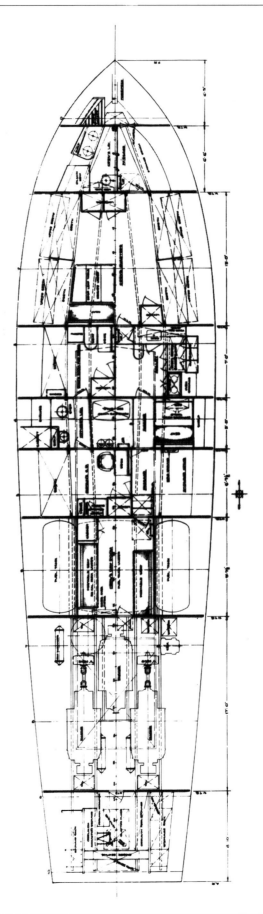

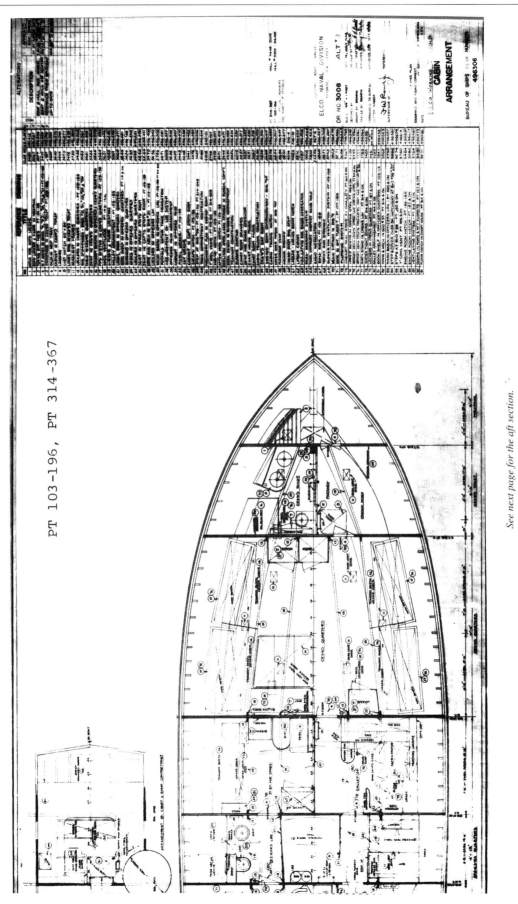

PT 103-196, PT 314-367

See next page for the aft section.

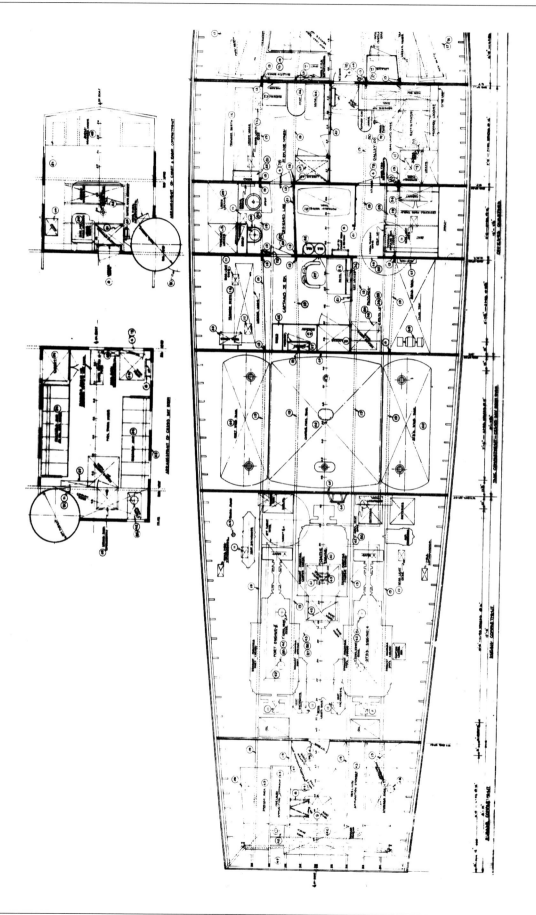

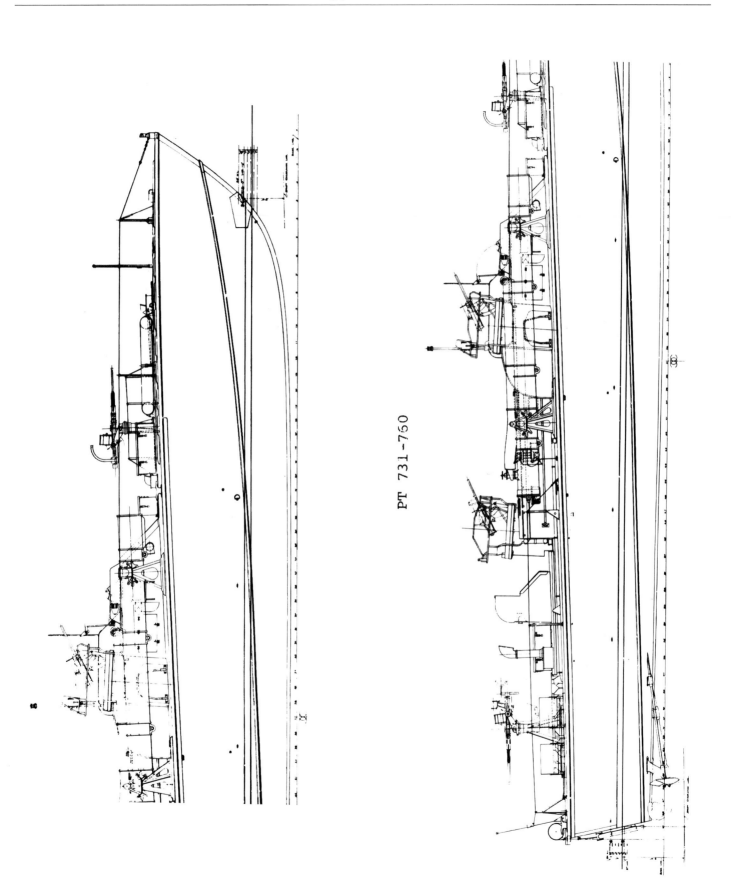

PT 731-750

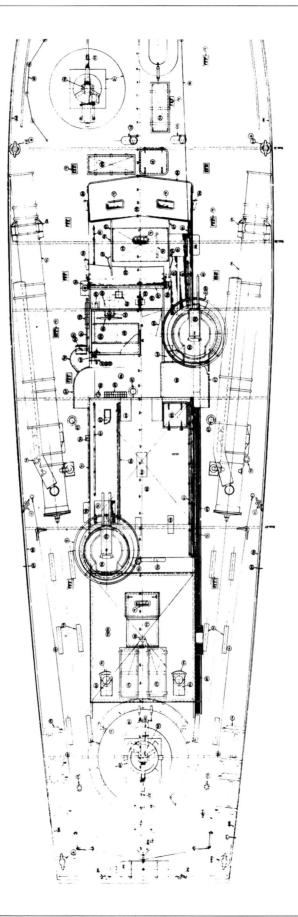

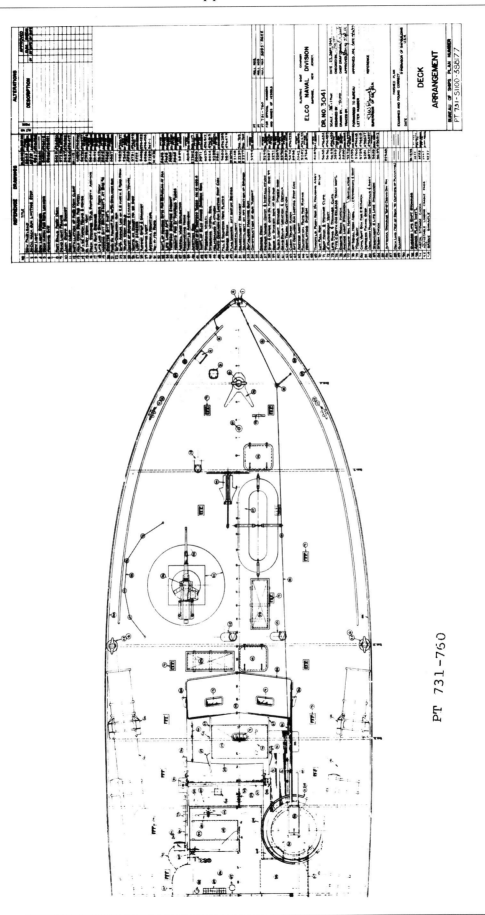

PT 731-760

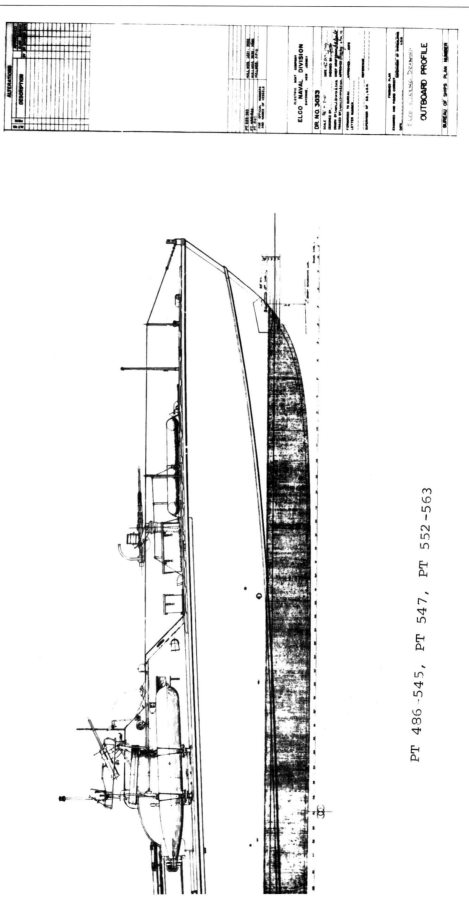

PT 486-545, PT 547, PT 552-563

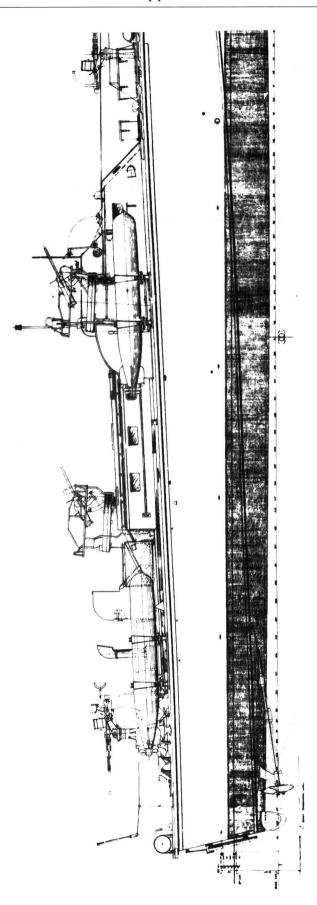

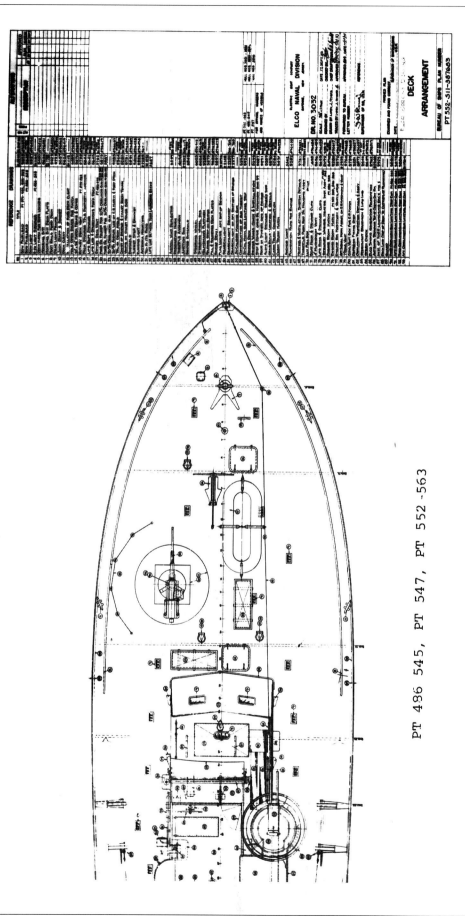

PT 486 545, PT 547, PT 552-563

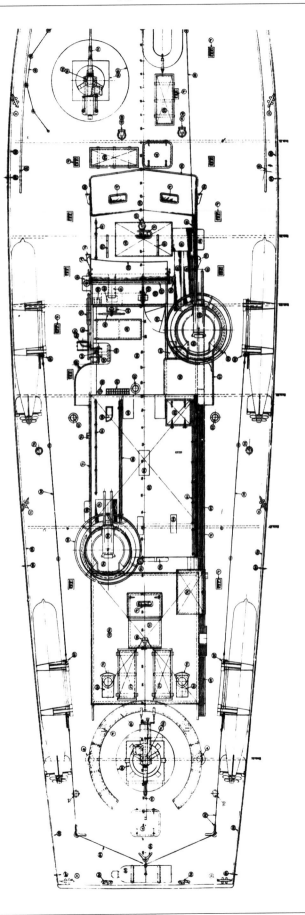

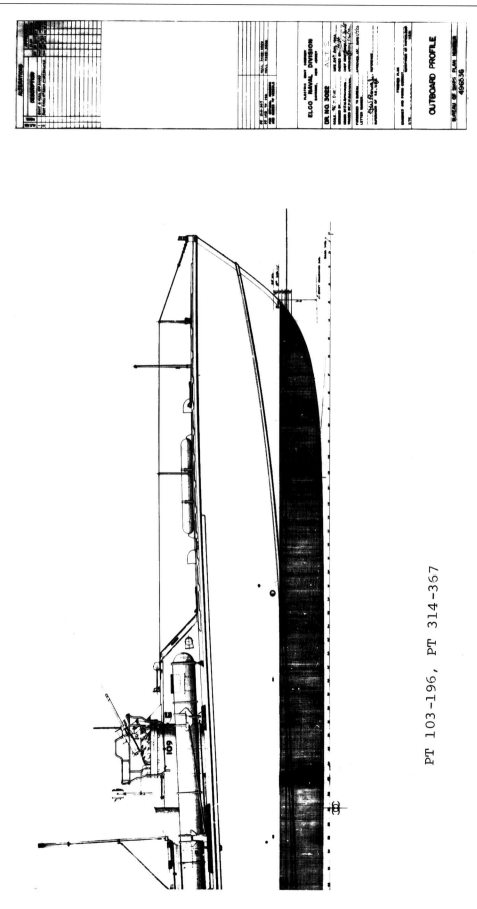

PT 103-196, PT 314-367

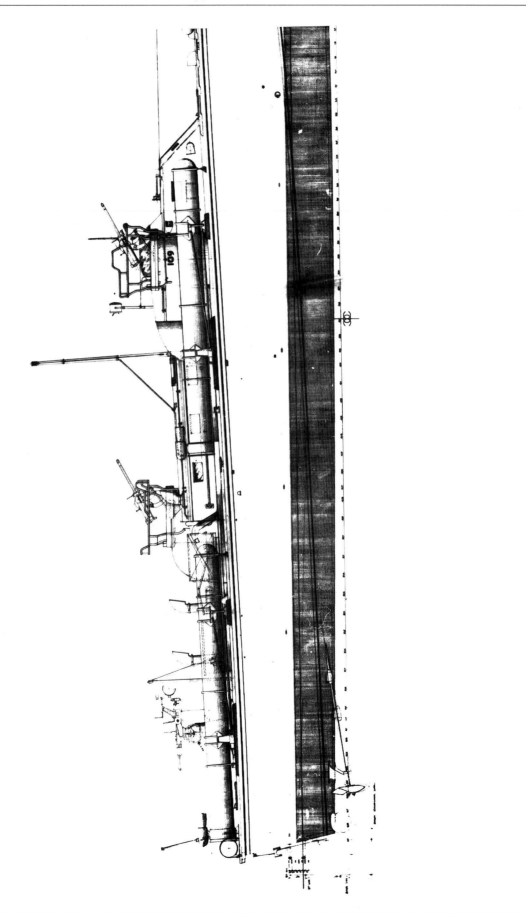

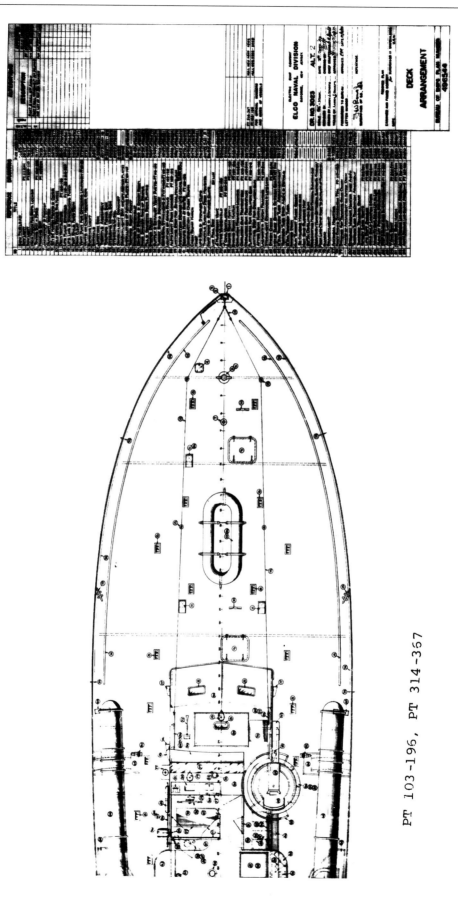

PT 103-196, PT 314-357

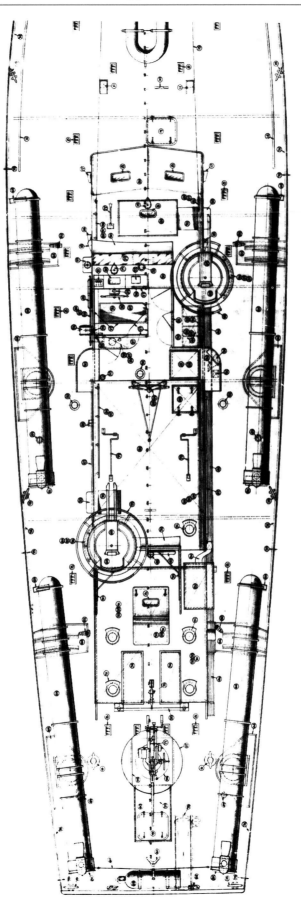

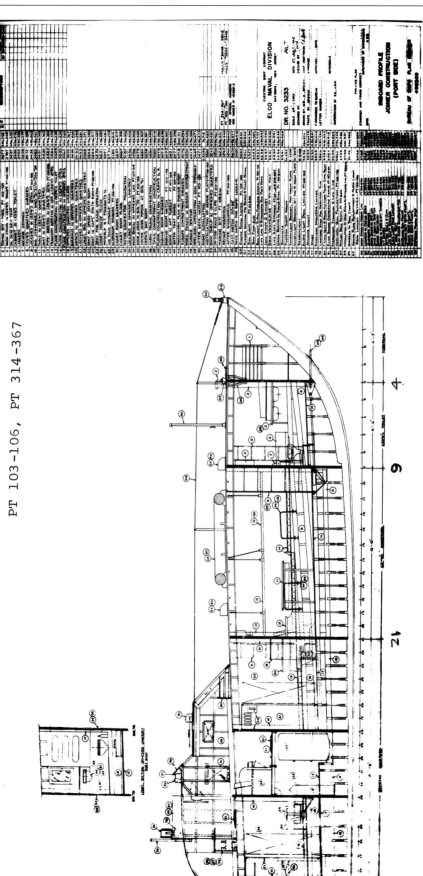

PT 103-106, PT 314-367

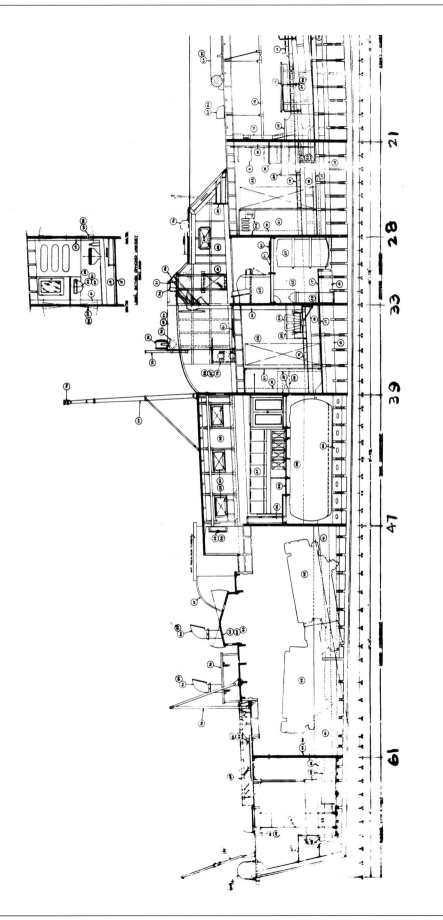

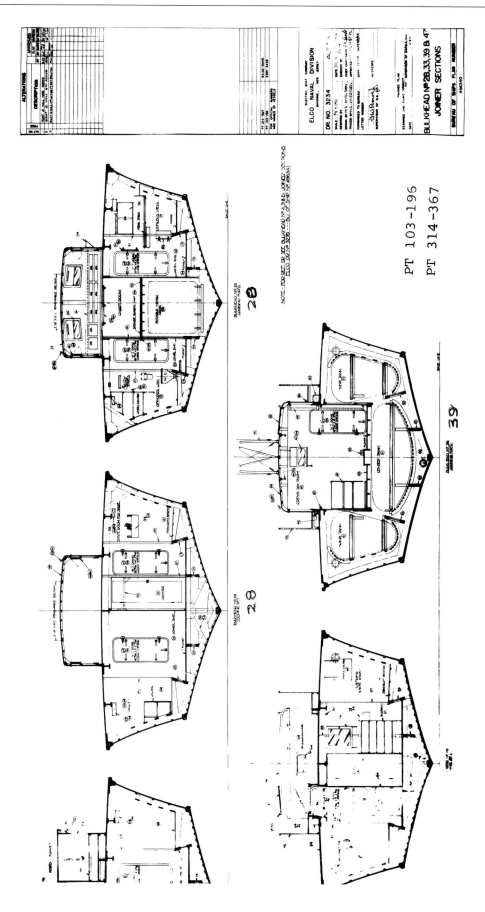

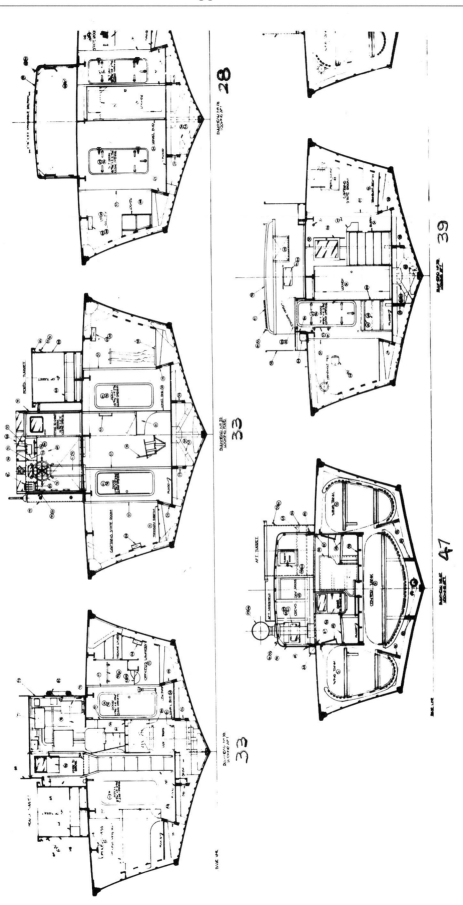

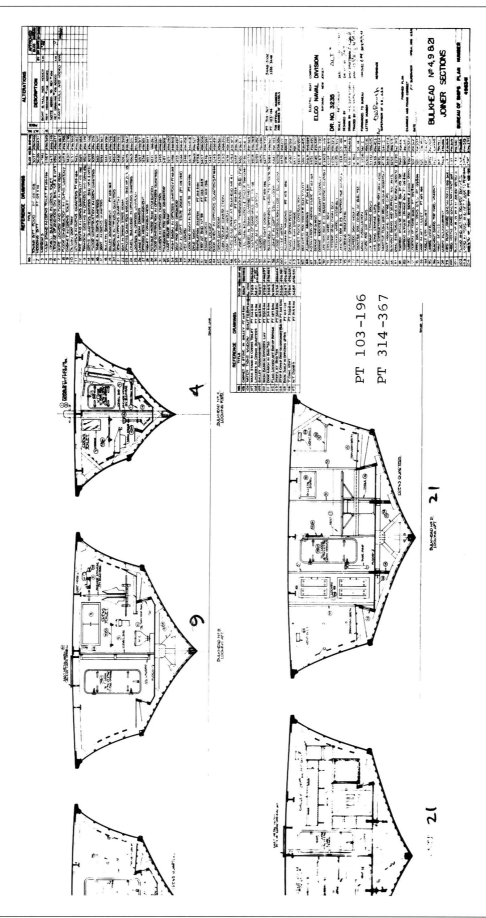

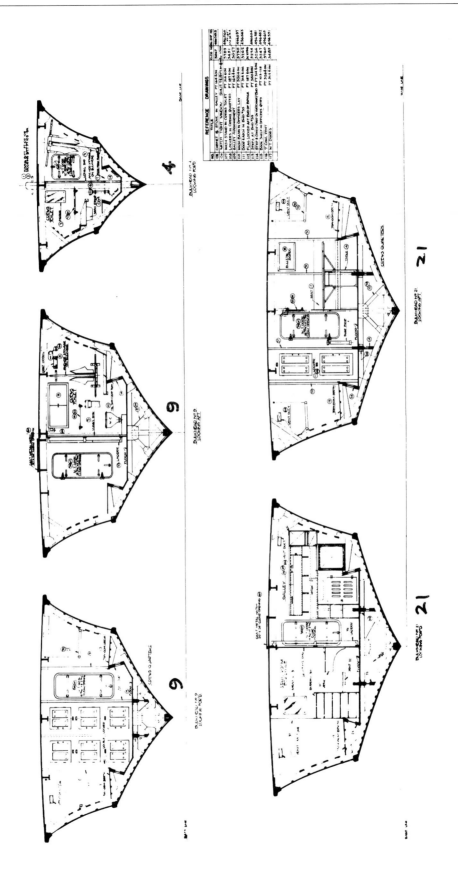

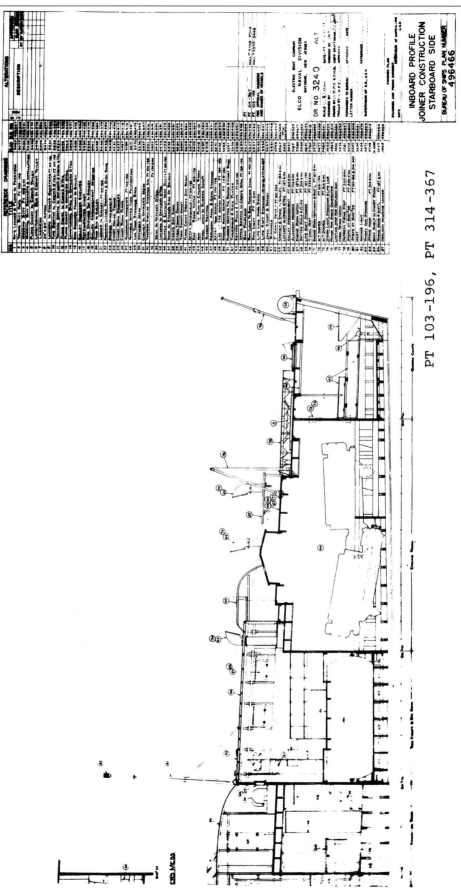

PT 103-196, PT 314-367

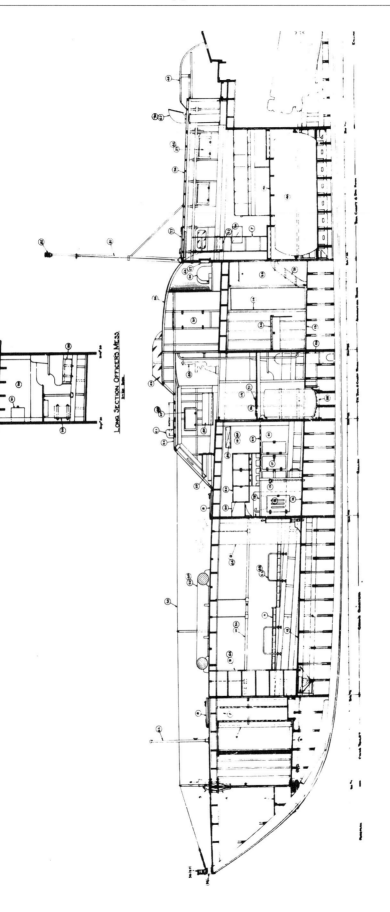

Long Section Officers Mess

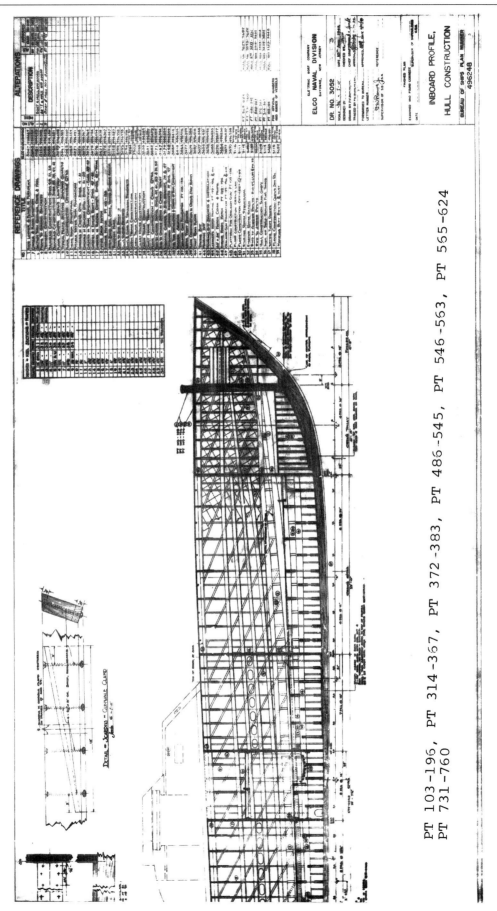

PT 103-196, PT 314-367, PT 372-383, PT 486-545, PT 546-563, PT 565-624
PT 731-760

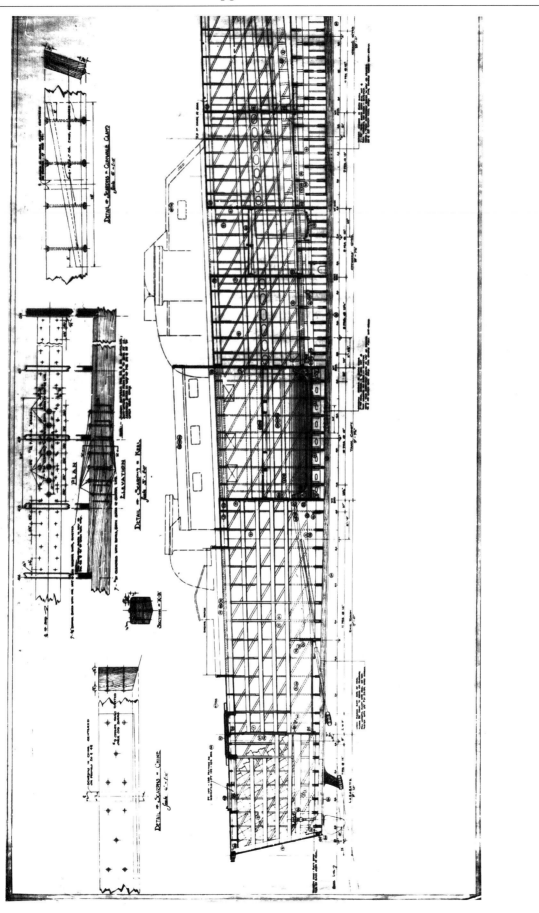

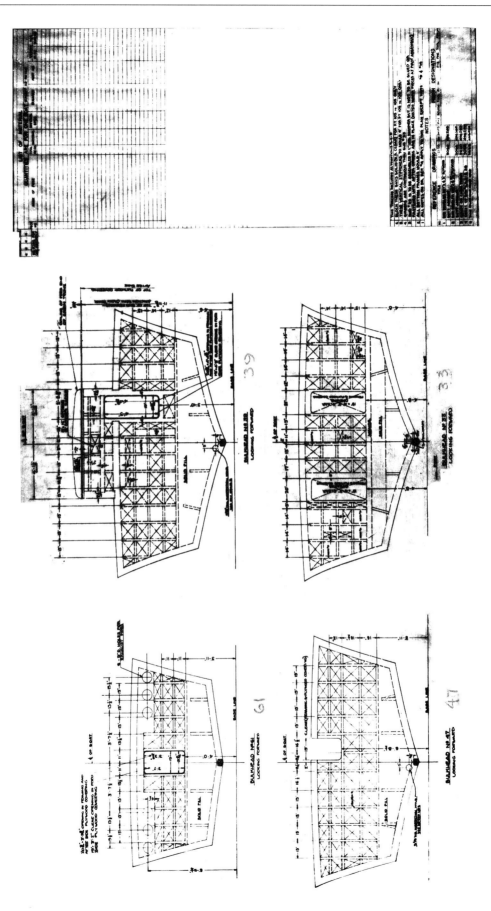

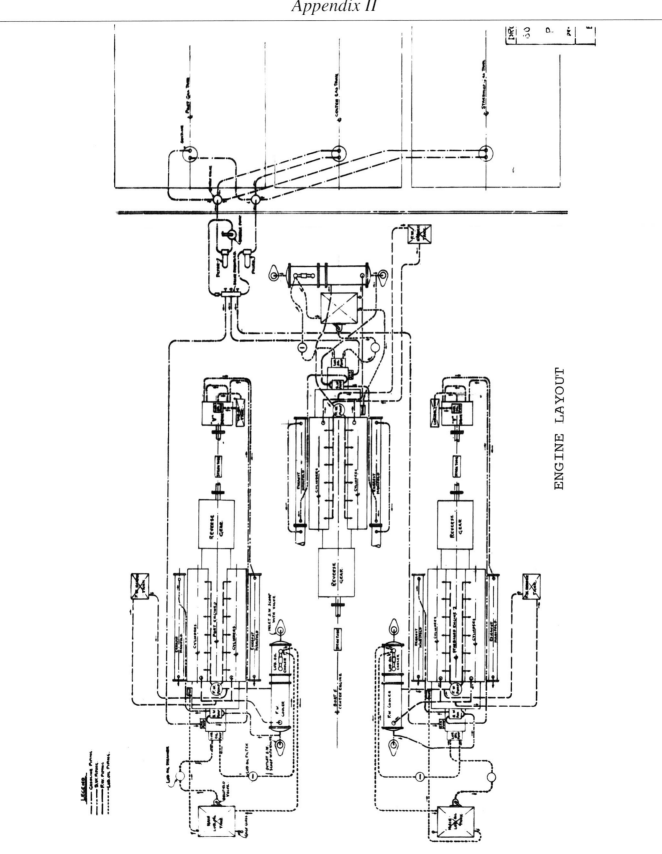

ENGINE LAYOUT

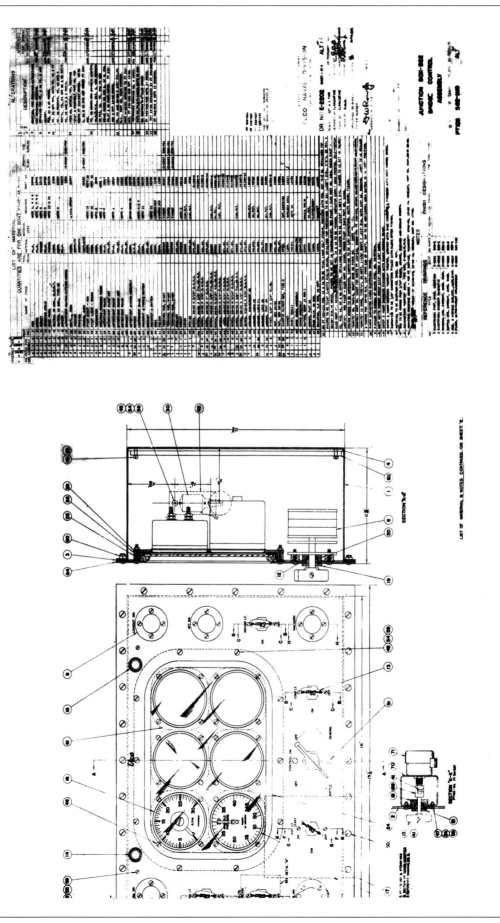

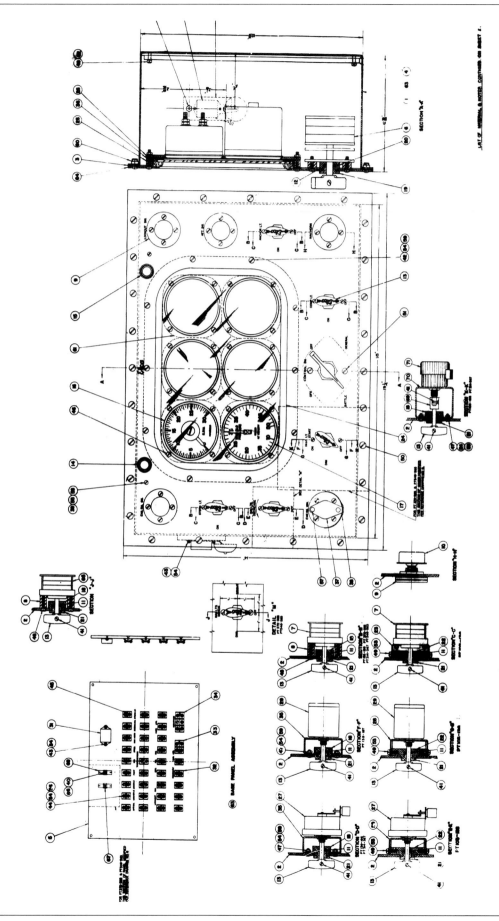

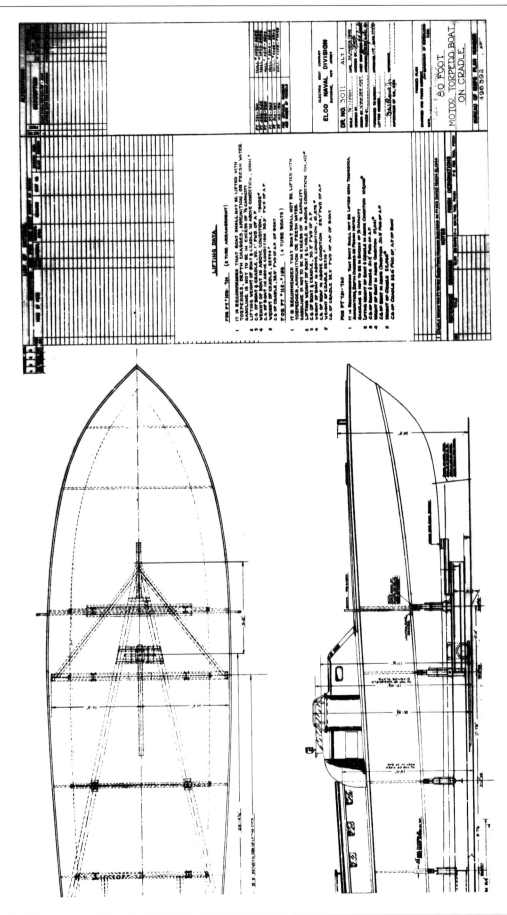

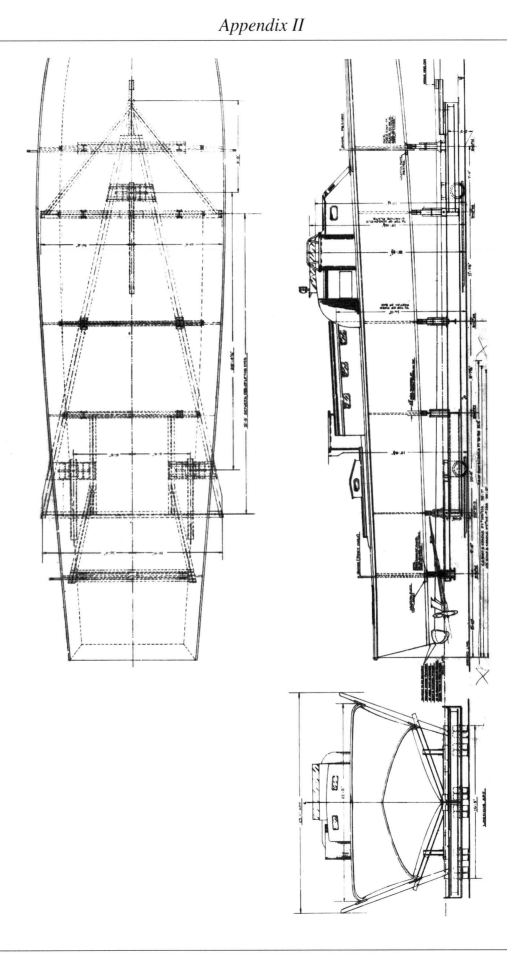

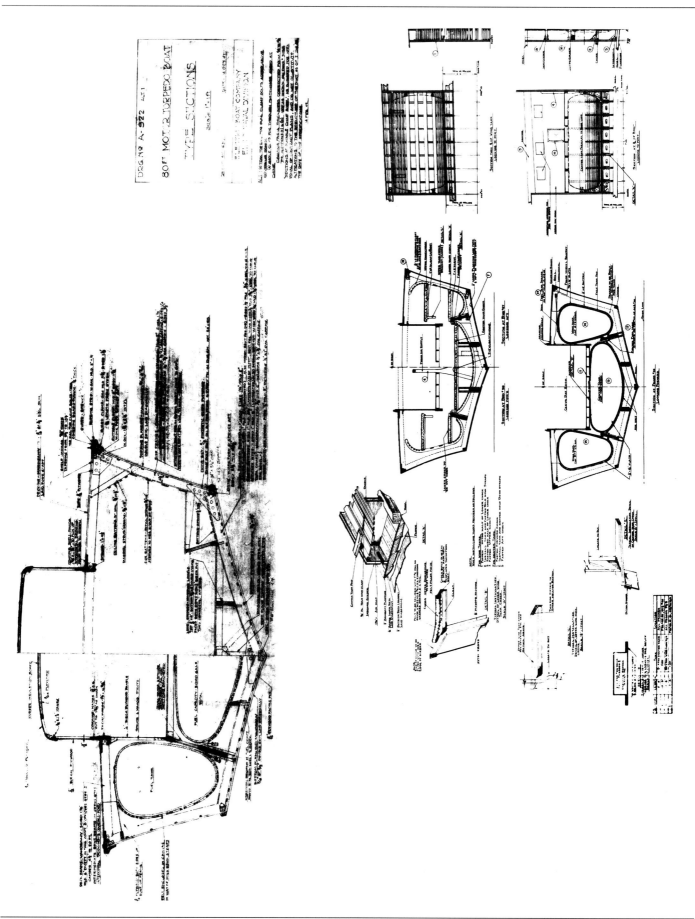

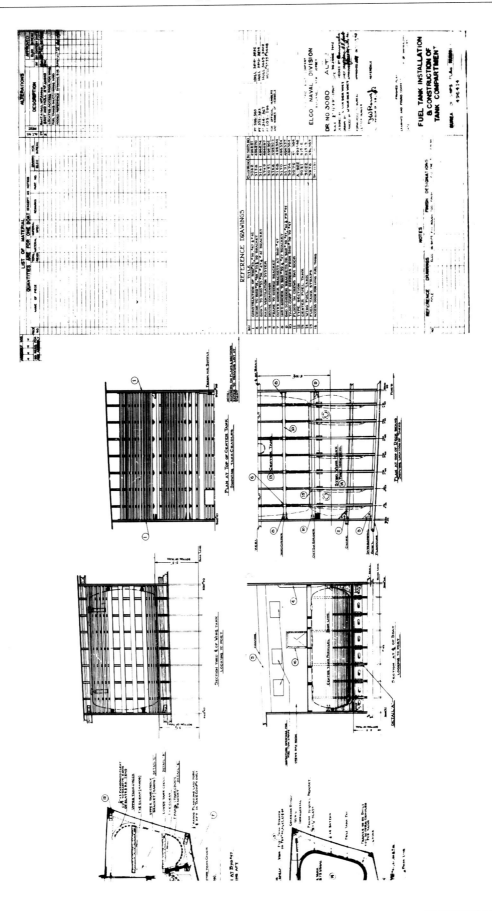

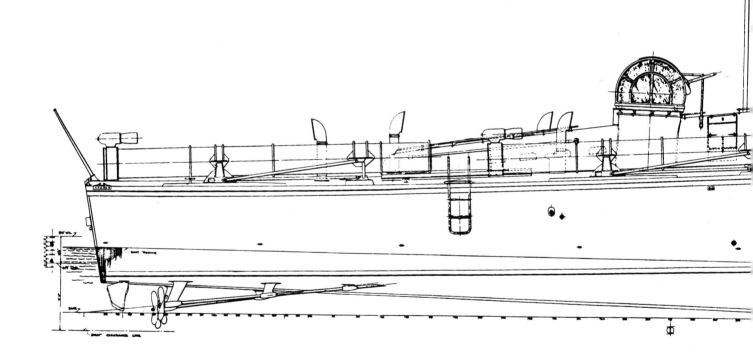

ELCO 77′   PT 20

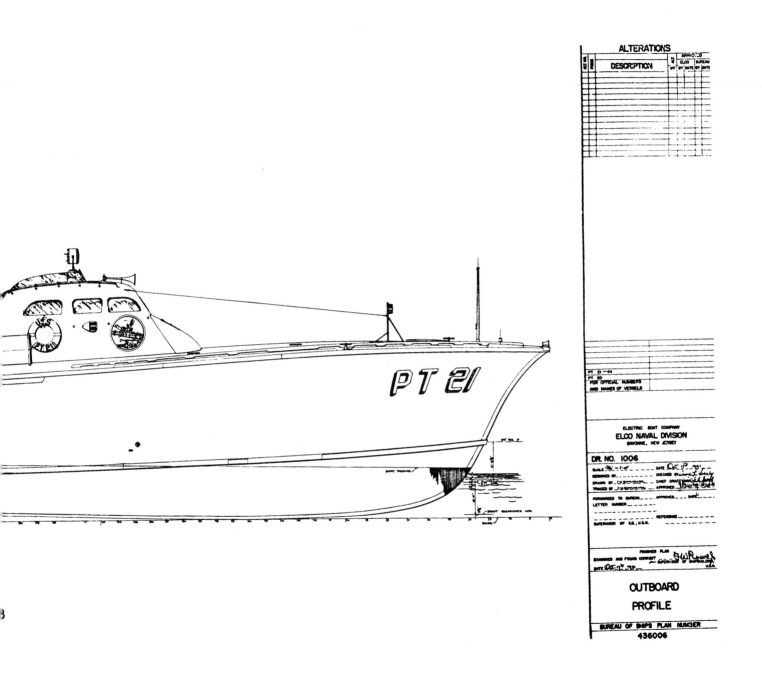

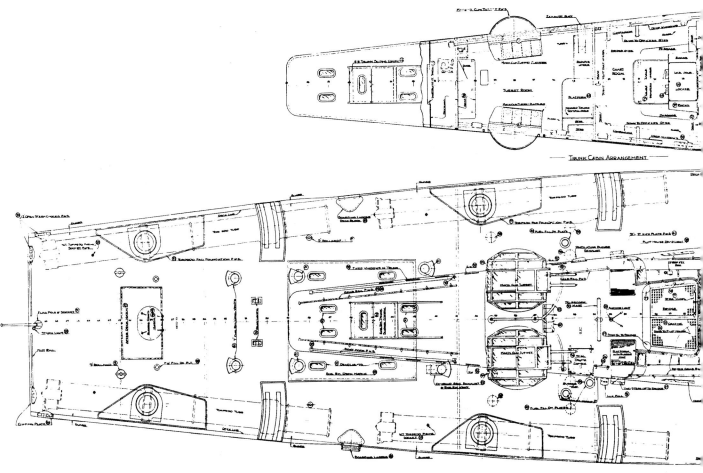

Trunk Cabin Arrangement

Deck Plan

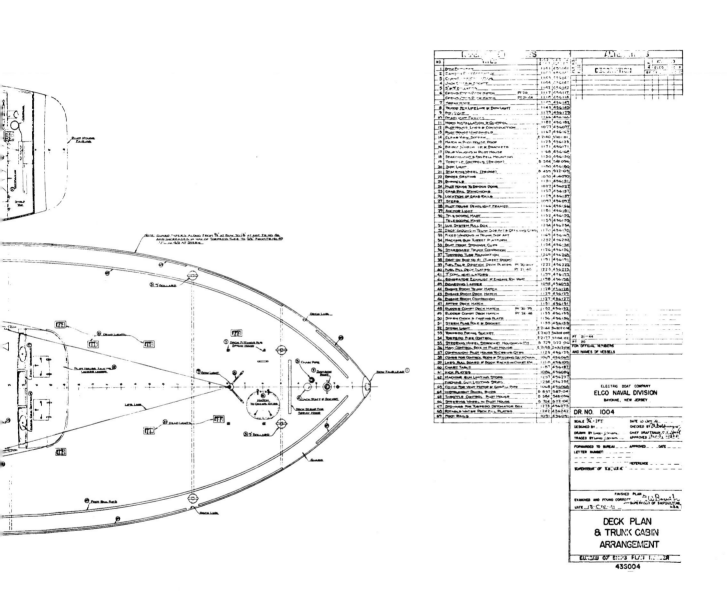

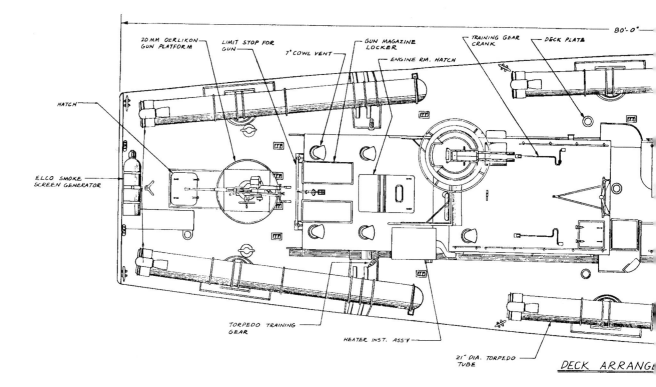

HATCH

20 MM OERLIKON
GUN PLATFORM

LIMIT STOP FOR
GUN

GUN MAGAZINE
LOCKER

7" COWL VENT

ENGINE RM. HATCH

TRAINING GEAR
CRANK

DECK PLATE

80'-0"

ELCO SMOKE
SCREEN GENERATOR

TORPEDO TRAINING
GEAR

HEATER INST. ASS'Y

21" DIA. TORPEDO
TUBE

DECK ARRANGE

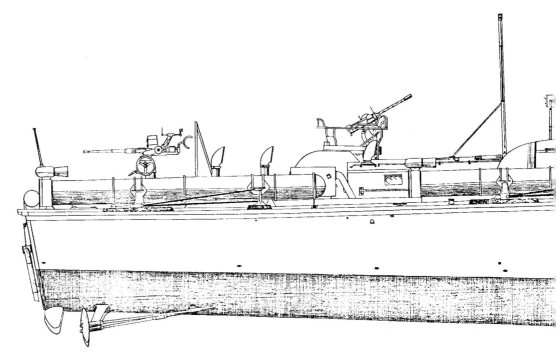

OUTBOARD PROF

ELCO 80' PT 103
BUILT FROM JUNE 1942 TO N

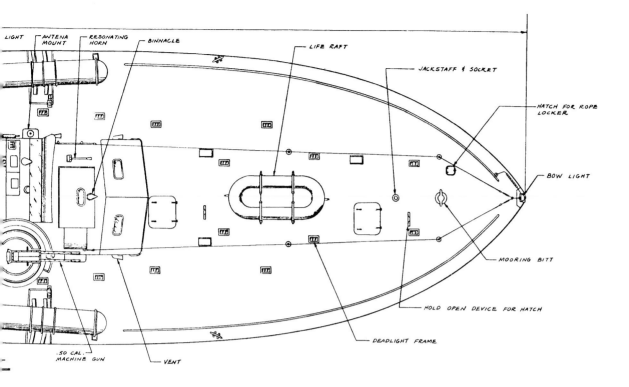

LIGHT — ANTENA MOUNT — RESONATING HORN — BINNACLE — LIFE RAFT — JACKSTAFF & SOCKET — HATCH FOR ROPE LOCKER — BOW LIGHT — MOORING BITT — HOLD OPEN DEVICE FOR HATCH — DEADLIGHT FRAME — .50 CAL. MACHINE GUN — VENT

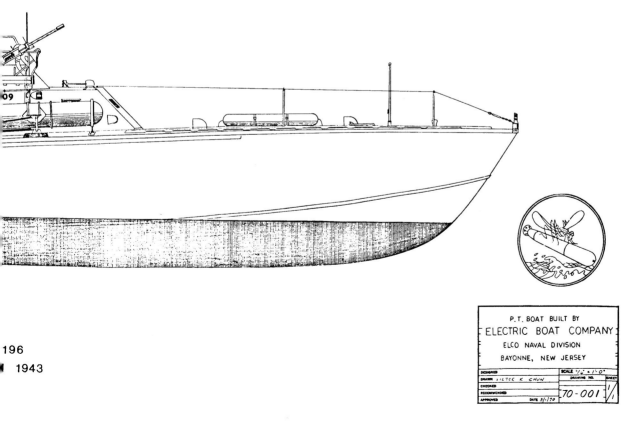

196

1943

P.T. BOAT BUILT BY
ELECTRIC BOAT COMPANY
ELCO NAVAL DIVISION
BAYONNE, NEW JERSEY

DESIGNED	SCALE ½" = 1'-0"	
DRAWN VICTOR K CHUN	DRAWING NO.	SHEET
CHECKED		
RECOMMENDED	70-001	1/1
APPROVED DATE 3/1/70		

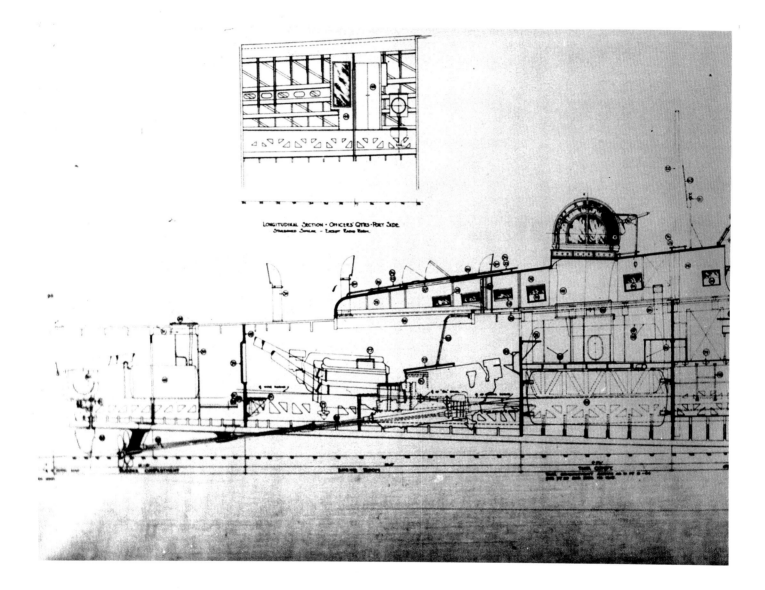

LONGITUDINAL SECTION · OFFICERS' QTRS · PORT SIDE
STARBOARD SIMILAR – EXCEPT RADIO ROOM.

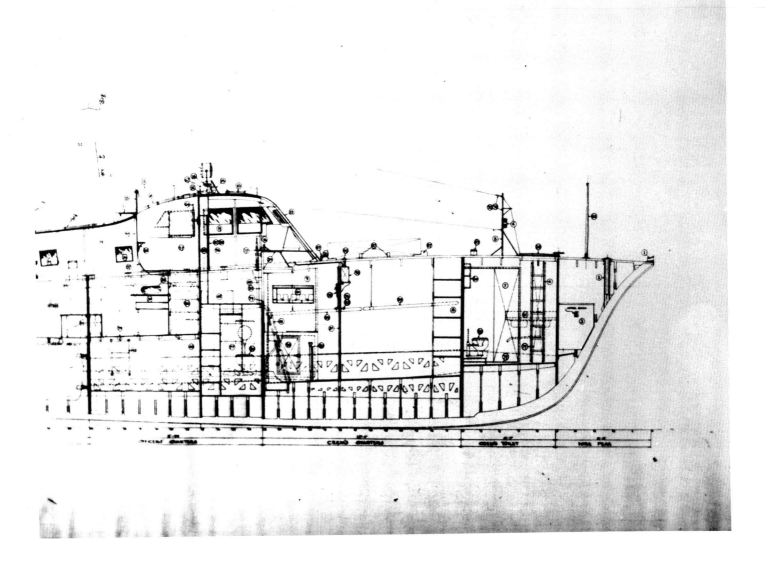

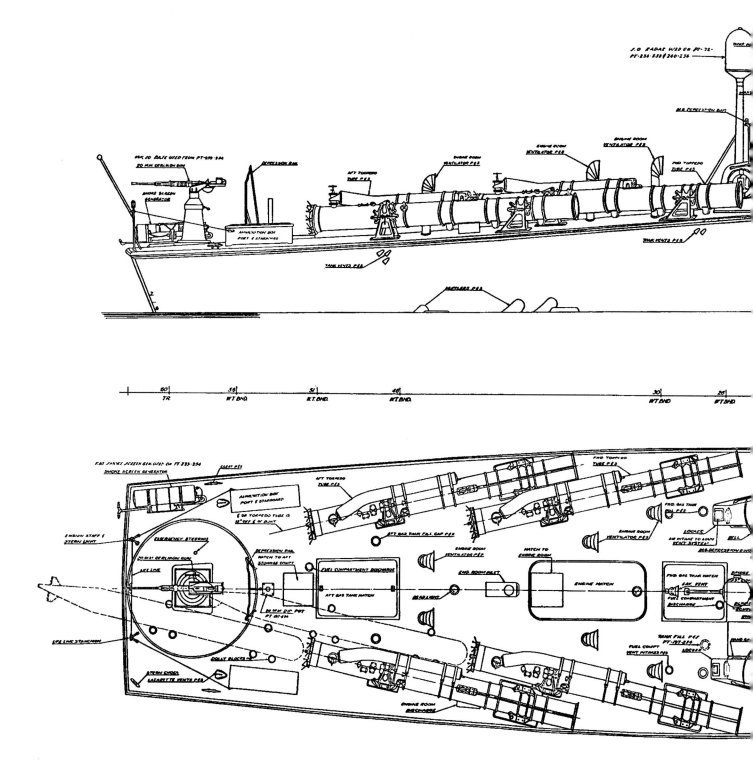

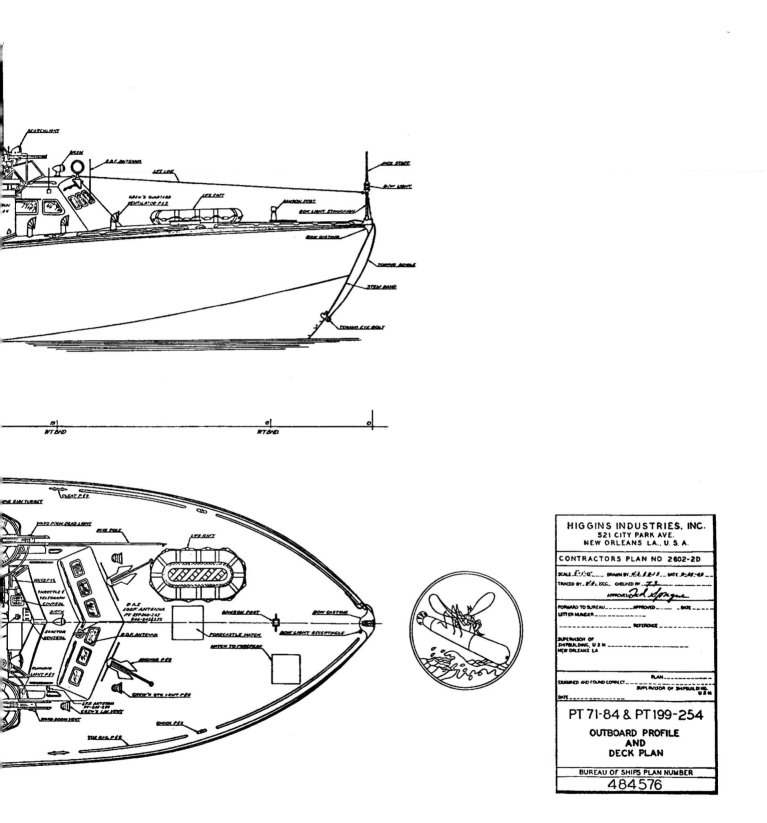

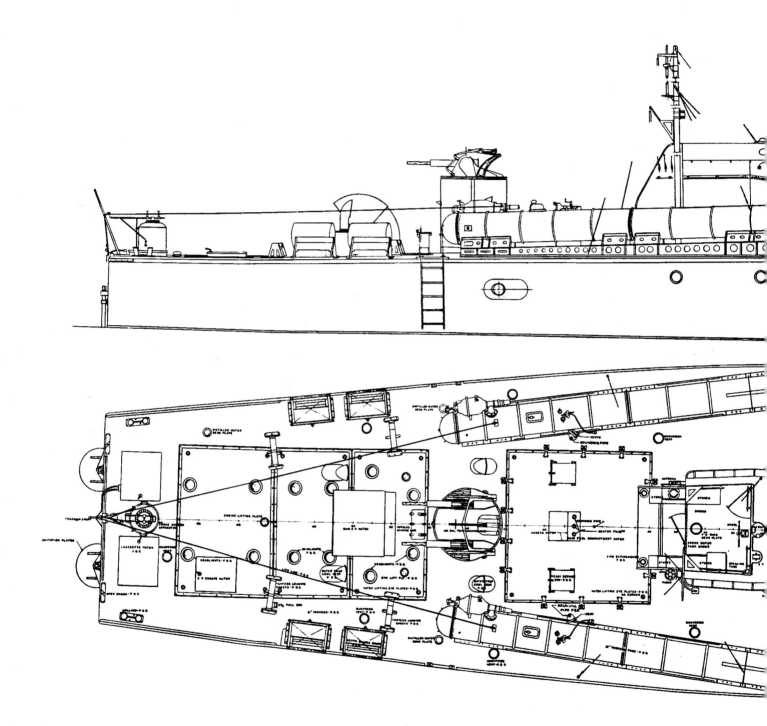

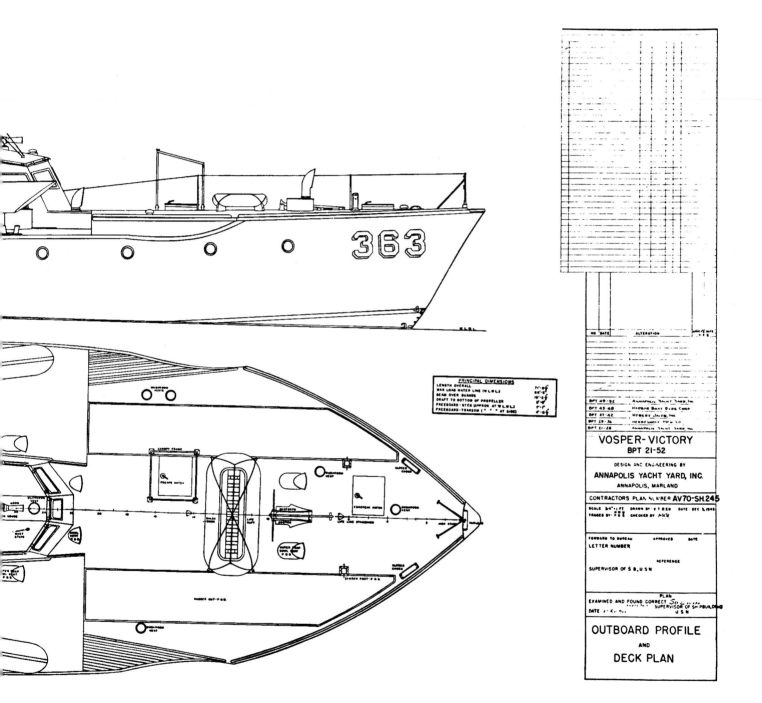

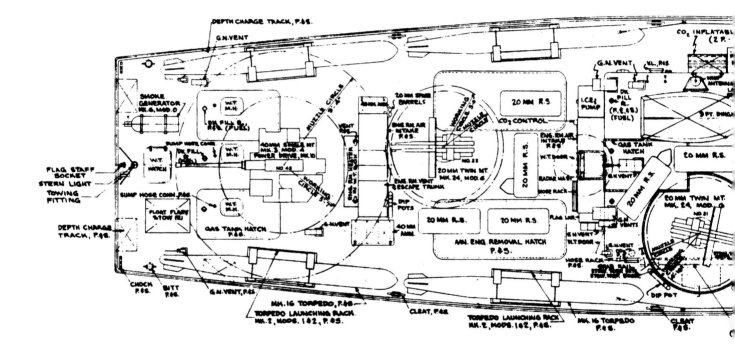

PT 810

ABBREVIATIONS

AMM.	AMMUNITION
ANT. FDN.	ANTENNA FOUNDATION
AUX.	AUXILIARY
₵.	CENTERLINE
DK.	DECK
ENG. RM.	ENGINE ROOM
G.N. VENT	GOOSENECK VENTILATOR
I.C.E.	INTERNAL COMBUSTION ENGINE
LKR.	LOCKER
M.H.	MANHOLE
MK.	MARK
MM.	MILLIMETER
MN. ENG.	MAIN ENGINE
MOD.	MODIFICATION
MT.	MOUNT
P.	PORT
R.	PLATE
P.P.I.	PLAN POSITION INDICATOR
R.S.	READY SERVICE
S.	STARBOARD
V.L.	VERTICAL LADDER
W.T.	WATERTIGHT
F.E.	FIRE EXTINGUISHER

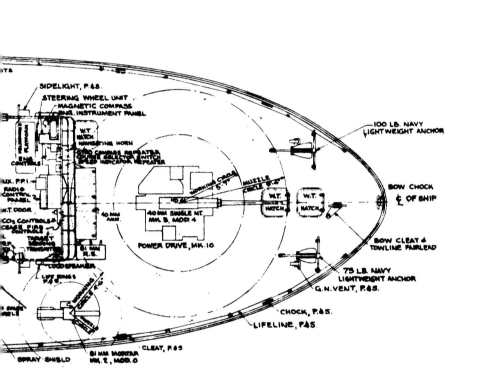

PT 810
MAIN DECK PLAN

BUREAU OF SHIPS BASIC NO. PT 810-S0103-105085

SCALE: 3/16"=1'-0"   SHEET NO. 6 OF 7

CREDIT: J. B. STEWART

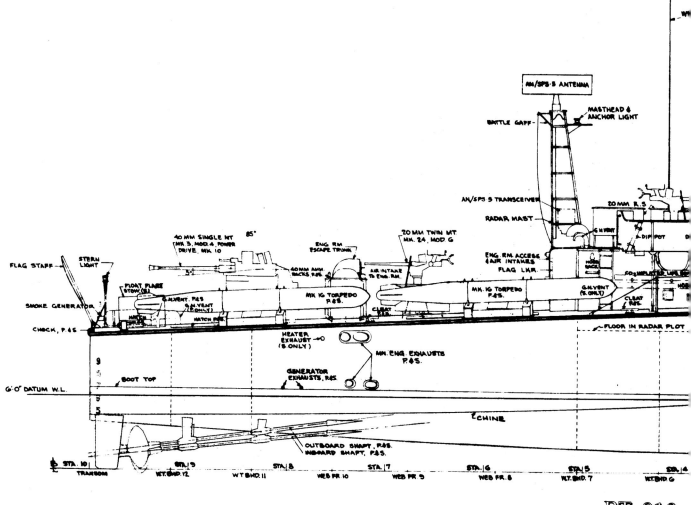

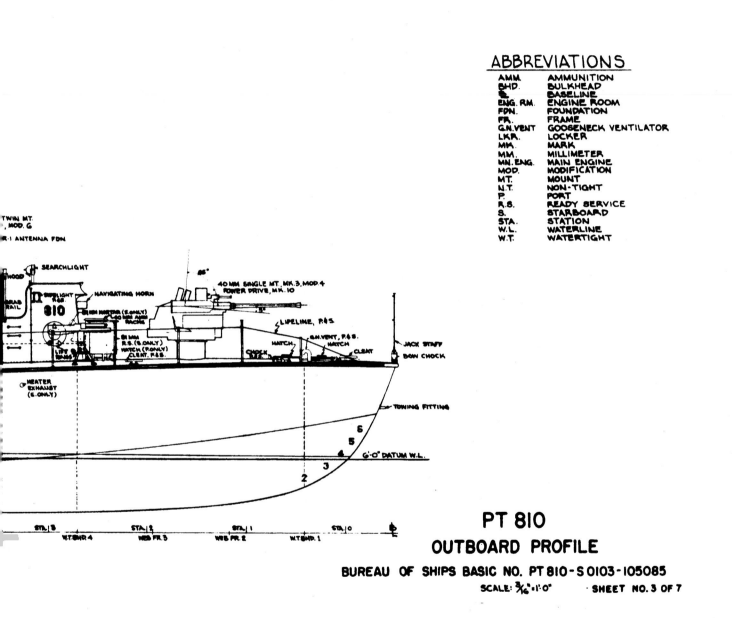

ABBREVIATIONS

AMM.	AMMUNITION
BHD.	BULKHEAD
℄	BASELINE
ENG. RM.	ENGINE ROOM
FDN.	FOUNDATION
FR.	FRAME
G.N.VENT.	GOOSENECK VENTILATOR
LKR.	LOCKER
MK.	MARK
MM.	MILLIMETER
MN. ENG.	MAIN ENGINE
MOD.	MODIFICATION
MT.	MOUNT
N.T.	NON-TIGHT
P.	PORT
R.S.	READY SERVICE
S.	STARBOARD
STA.	STATION
W.L.	WATERLINE
W.T.	WATERTIGHT

PT 810
OUTBOARD PROFILE

BUREAU OF SHIPS BASIC NO. PT 810-S 0103-105085

SCALE: 3/16"=1'-0"   · SHEET NO. 3 OF 7

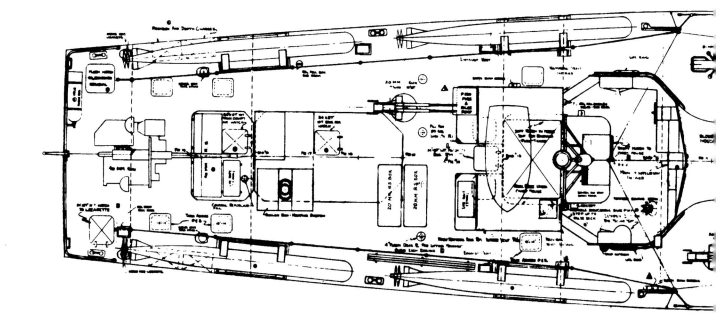

PT 81

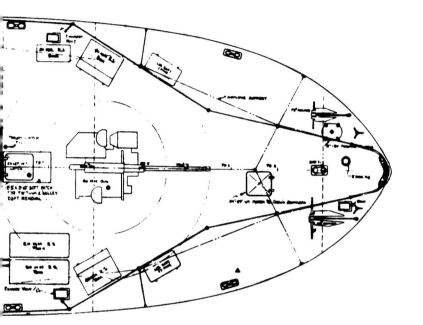

PT- 811

MAIN DECK PLAN

BUREAU OF SHIPS BASIC NO.   PT 811- 30103- 965168

SCALE 3/16"= 1'— 0"   SHEET 6 OF 7

CREDIT: J. B. STEWART

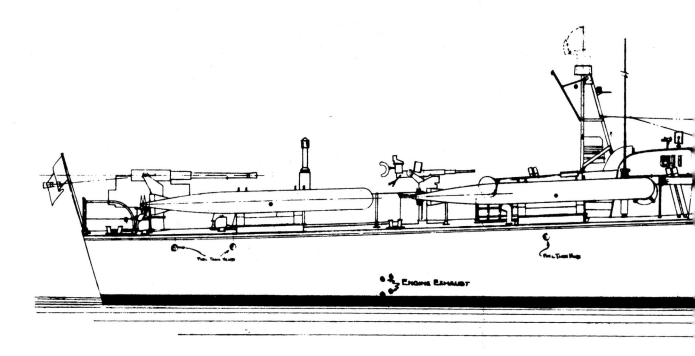

PT 811

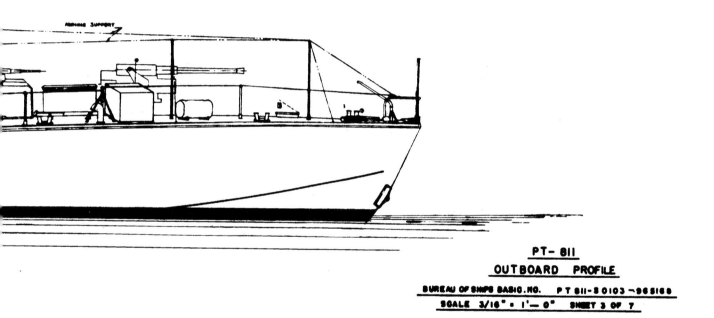

PT- 811

OUTBOARD PROFILE

BUREAU OF SHIPS BASIC.NO.   PT 811-S 0103 -965168

SCALE 3/16" = 1'— 0"   SHEET 3 OF 7

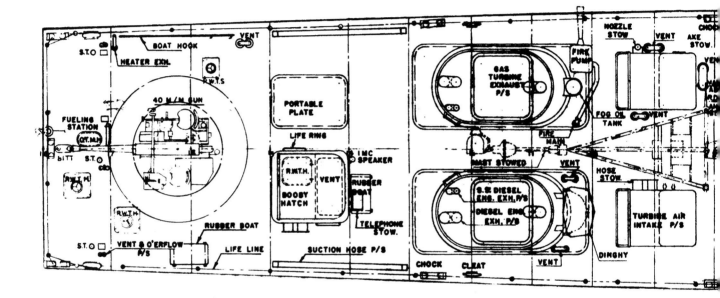

PT 812

PLATE 5

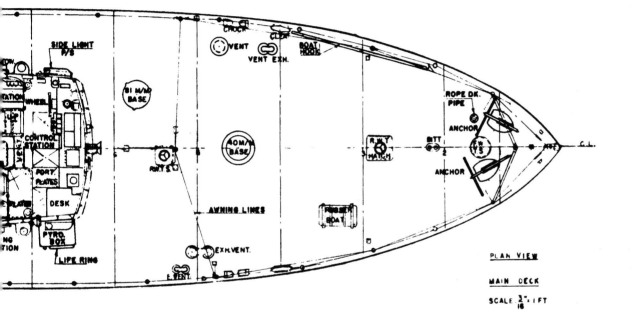

PLAN VIEW

MAIN DECK

SCALE $\frac{3}{16}$" = 1 FT

BUSHIP NO PT 812 - $\frac{800}{50103}$ - 1740745

CREDIT: J. B. STEWART

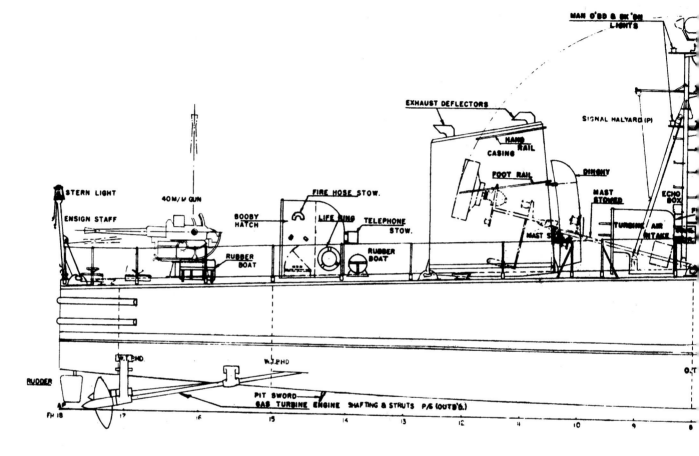

STERN LIGHT

ENSIGN STAFF

40 M/M GUN

RUBBER BOAT

BOOBY HATCH

FIRE HOSE STOW.

LIFE RING

TELEPHONE STOW.

RUBBER BOAT

EXHAUST DEFLECTORS

HAND RAIL

CASING

FOOT RAIL

DINGHY

MAST STOWED

MAST S

MAN O'BD & BK 'DN LIGHTS

SIGNAL HALYARD (P)

ECHO BOX

TURBINE AIR INTAKE

RUDDER

W.T. BHD.

W.T. BHD.

O.T.

PIT SWORD

GAS TURBINE ENGINE SHAFTING & STRUTS P/S (OUTB'6.)

FR 18   17   16   15   14   13   12   11   10   9   8

PT 812

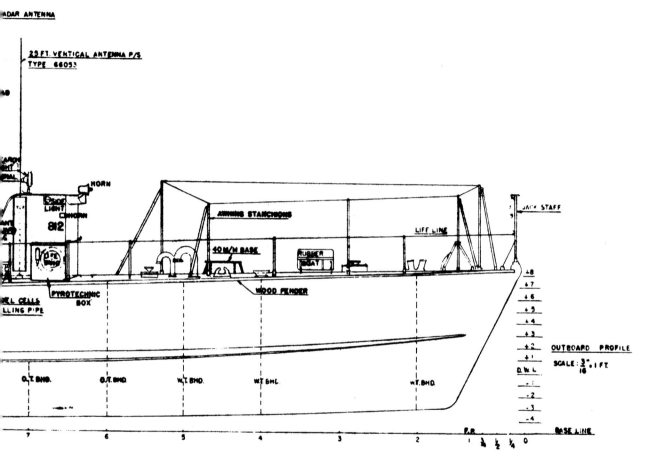

RADAR ANTENNA

25 FT. VERTICAL ANTENNA P/S
TYPE 66053

HORN

LIGHT

812

OUTBOARD PROFILE

SCALE: $\frac{3}{16}$ = 1 FT.

AWNING STANCHIONS

JACK STAFF

LIFE LINE

40 M/M BASE

RUBBER BOAT

WOOD FENDER

PYROTECHNIC BOX

CELLS
LLING PIPE

+8
+7
+6
+5
+4
+3
+2
+1
D.W.L.
-1
-2
-3
-4

BASE LINE

O.T. BHD.   O.T. BHD.   W.T. BHD.   W.T. BHD.   W.T. BHD.

7   6   5   4   3   2   F.R.   0

BUSHIPS NO. PT812-800/60103-1740745

CREDIT: J. B. STEWART

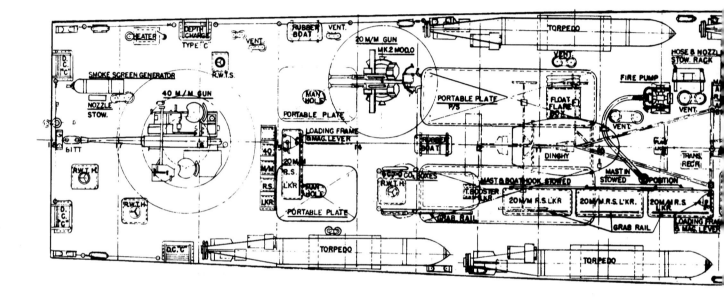

PT 812

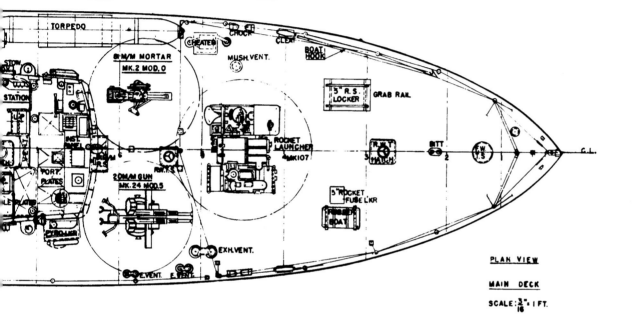

PLATE 5

TORPEDO

8 M/M MORTAR
MK.2 MOD.0

MUSH. VENT.

CREATED

CHOCK

CLEAT

BOAT HOOK

3" R.S. LOCKER

GRAB RAIL

STATION

INST. PANEL

20M/M GUN
MK.24 MOD.5

ROCKET LAUNCHER
MK107

R.W. HATCH

BTT
2

F.W.
V.S.

C.L.

PORT. PLATES

5" ROCKET FUSE L'KR

EXH. VENT.

E. VENT.   E. VENT.

PLAN VIEW

MAIN DECK

SCALE: $\frac{3}{16}$" = I FT.

BUSHIP NO. PT 812-S0103-958324

CREDIT: J. B. STEWART

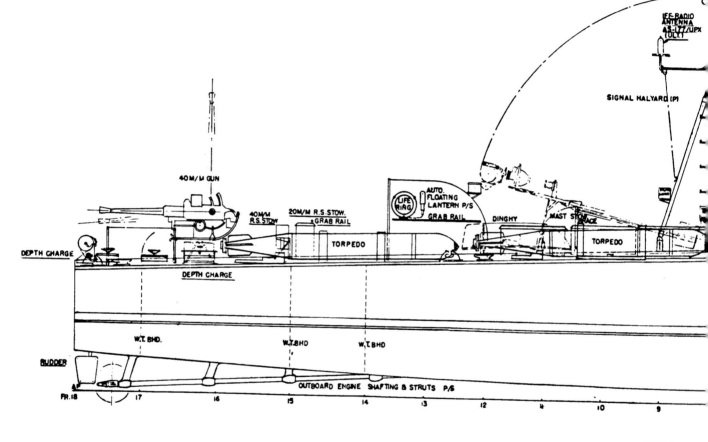

40 M/M GUN

DEPTH CHARGE

DEPTH CHARGE

40M/M R.S. STOW

20M/M R.S. STOW.
GRAB RAIL

TORPEDO

LIFE RING

AUTO. FLOATING LANTERN P/S

GRAB RAIL

DINGHY

MAST STORAGE

TORPEDO

IFF RADIO ANTENNA AS-177/UPX (ULY)

SIGNAL HALYARD (P)

RUDDER

W.T. BHD.

W.T.BHD.

W.T BHD

FR.18   17   16   15   14   13   12   11   10   9

OUTBOARD ENGINE SHAFTING & STRUTS P/S

PT 812

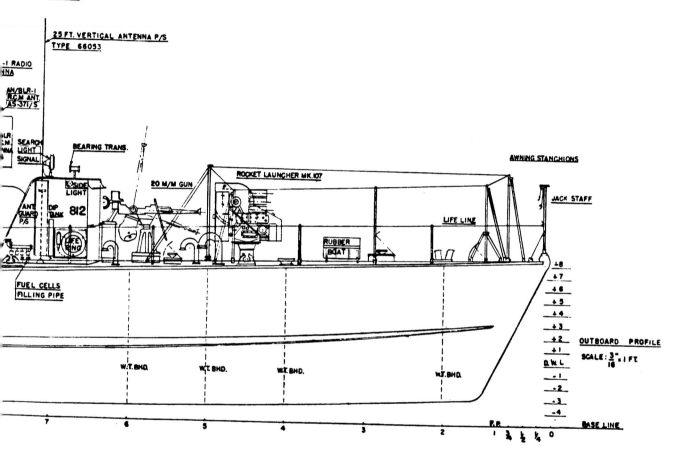

PS-5 RADAR ANTENNA

25 FT. VERTICAL ANTENNA P/S
TYPE 66053

-I RADIO
NNA

AN/BLR-I
RLCM ANT.
AS-371/S

LR
M
NNA

SEARCH
LIGHT
SIGNAL

BEARING TRANS.

AWNING STANCHIONS

JACK STAFF

SIDE
LIGHT

812

ROCKET LAUNCHER MK.107

20 M/M GUN

LIFE LINE

ANT
GUARD
P/S

DIP
TANK

LIFE
RING

RUBBER
BOAT

FUEL CELLS
FILLING PIPE

+8
+7
+6
+5
+4
+3
+2
+1
B.W.L
-1
-2
-3
-4

OUTBOARD PROFILE

SCALE: 3/16 = 1 FT

W.T. BHD.   W.T. BHD.   W.T. BHD.   W.T. BHD.

7   6   5   4   3   2   P.P.   BASE LINE
                                                    1 3/4 1/2 1/4 0

CREDIT: J.B. STEWART BUSHIPS NO. PT812-SO103-958324

Note the early radar dome. Courtesy of Sea Classics.

"Knight of the Sea" War time poster by ELCO. Courtesy of PT Boat Museum.

This painting is by Harold Garland and shows MTB 309 of the 15th MTB Flotilla under Lt. Denis Jarmain. MTB 309 participated in a raid against Tobruk in September, 1942. Coutesy of Harold Garland.

APPENDIX III
Postwar History of Higgins Industries and Elco

Higgins Industries:

Higgins Industries came out of the war with $5 million plant facilities that employed 13000 men and women. In addition to PT boats, they also built landing craft (LCPs, LCPLs, LCVPs, LCMs). By November, 1945, the work force was reduced to 2500. Andrew J. Higgins, fed up with the problems with the War Labor Board, the National Labor Relation board, and the union trouble, decided to close the 21 plants. His dream of employing 30000 workers in postwar manufacturing had become a nightmare. While he started to liquate the company in January, 1945, he concluded a $10 million financing arrangement with the New York investment house of Van Alstyne, Noel & Co. under which a new company, Higgins, Inc. was formed financed by a public sale of stocks. Higgins, Inc. had speculate in several new ventures but proved unsuccessful.

Andrew J. Higgins died on August 1, 1952. The helm was passed over to his son, Andrew, Jr. (president), Frank (vice president), Roland (development), Edward (assistance plant superentendent).

Higgins, Inc. changed to Higco, Inc. on December 13, 1955 and then liquadated for the benefit of the creditor on March 23, 1966 with no stockholders' equity.

Elco:

During the war, the Elco facility in Bayone, N.J. built 399 PT boats with more than 3000 men and women working three shifts a day, six days a week. Six consecutive Navy "E" were awarded to Elco for defense contracting excellence. The last boat, PT 622, was delivered to the Navy from the Elco plant in Bayonne, NJ, on October 25, 1945.

After the war, its extensive manufacturing plants and the huge production capabilities were now useless overhead when the postwar demand for pleasure boats had decreased. At the end of 1949, Elco closed its gate for the last time and becane a division of General Dynamic. For 37 years the company lain dormant until Joseph W. Fleming acquired the Elco name, moved the company to Highland, N.J., and started making electric marine propulsion systems and electric launches. Elco was once again a builder of boats.

In 1988, Charles Houghton and his former Harvard classmate, Bill Foster, bought the company for they believed it is time for the Elco electric boats to make a comeback due to the enviromental soundness of the electrically power system. The company has built 50 boats since December 1995 as compared to one PT boat every 60 hours during the height of World War II production. The company is currently upgrading its facilities for the Elco name still has a following.

APPENDIX IV
PT Boat "Insignias" of WWII Operating Squadrons

Courtesy of PT Boat Museum.

Also from the publisher